Anna E. (Anna Elizabeth) Dickinson

A Ragged Register

Of People, Places and Opinions

Anna E. (Anna Elizabeth) Dickinson
A Ragged Register
Of People, Places and Opinions

ISBN/EAN: 9783744652612

Printed in Europe, USA, Canada, Australia, Japan

Cover: Foto ©ninafisch / pixelio.de

More available books at **www.hansebooks.com**

A RAGGED REGISTER

(OF PEOPLE PLACES AND OPINIONS)

BY

ANNA E. DICKINSON

NEW YORK
HARPER & BROTHERS, PUBLISHERS
FRANKLIN SQUARE
1879

Entered according to Act of Congress, in the year 1879, by
HARPER & BROTHERS,
In the Office of the Librarian of Congress, at Washington.

TO

MY MOTHER

FOR WHOSE ENTERTAINMENT THE MANUSCRIPT OF THIS BOOK WAS ORIGINALLY PENNED

I Dedicate the Printed Volume

A RAGGED REGISTER.

I.

I WANT to go somewhere away from city walls and sewer smells and "L" abominations. Of that I am sure—but *where?*

"Where?" did I hear you, my invisible friend, echo? "Where! Why there are *fifty* places——"

Yes; I know. Unluckily, it is the things you *don't* want that are always accessible.

Let me consider. Let me sit down and ponder for a space over the ragged register of times and places that in some sort has been kept by my brain. A shabby-looking book, mutilated and half effaced, still it may help me from stand-still to action and—who knows?—serve as a bit of amusement to you by the way.

Shall we go a-fishing? No. To the sea? No. To the springs? No. Is it to the mountains we will wend? If so, by which path and to what ending?

It shall not be the Adirondacks, since I am sufficiently a sybarite to object to smoke and gnats and to look with disfavor upon manifold wettings with an insufficiency of drying sunshine.

Nor yet the White Hills. If they were lying under an autumn sun they would be tempting, but now—— ?

Times a many have I made my pilgrimage to this summer shrine in summer weather, only to sneeze and shiver through dreary days and weeks, and leave with a strong determination to do penance nevermore ; and yet have been tempted by renewed seasons to repeated efforts and exasperating disappointments.

Twenty-seven times had I gazed from the summit of Mount Washington at tossing clouds and sombre or ghostly mists, when the resplendent beauty of a summer morning tempted me to a tenth foot expedition and twenty-eighth ascent.

To be sure, if there is "luck in odd numbers" and the converse is also true, I had but an ill showing—but what of that! "He either fears his fate too much or his deserts are small" who does not dare much and also dare often.

With humility I have decided that, in this case

at least, my deserts are small. Doubtless I had too often scoffed at what this height could reveal to receive from it even justice, and certainly to be deemed unworthy of any display of generosity.

As I and my stick went our way to the mountain's base, the air was crystal clear. Crystal clear it remained as I tramped over the miles that wind through the trees dwarfed and tempest scarred. Crystal clear was its mood when—the woods abandoned, the scrub pines left behind, the last straggling spear of dreary vegetation vanished—the skirmish across the bleak ledges began.

Now or never! thought I, as I tramped out on the first of these. If the air *stays* clear I will abjure my heresies and subscribe to the faith of those who believe that New England mountains are to be reckoned in the same catalogue of saints as those that lift their solemn majesties toward the heavenly azure of the western skies.

I trudged along in a desperate faith, born perhaps of hope, certainly not of experience, and directly plunged into the soft fuzz of a nebulous cloud, and plunged out of it into chastened sunshine.

Up and down drifted mists and vapors lovely enough in themselves, and objects to be admired, had I not had a surfeit of them in past times; but, here and there, as I paused at this or that ledge, some such royal views broke upon the vision as to assure me of imperial splendor at the mountain-top.

Alas for faith and hope together! When within two miles of the summit I fell into the close embrace of wind and cloud—and liked not the companionship.

Not a foot could I see from me, around, above, below. No rain fell, but the clouds penetrated garments and body together till both felt sodden. The wind flapped and veered, blowing not from one quarter, nor yet as from a distance, but slapping and striking, now on face, now on feet, in chest or back or side as with a solitary hand of some huge creature who stood close to play his painful pranks, and in an instant vanished to assail from fresh vantage ground.

Long before the cone was reached, giant and pranks had fled. The air was dense and dark to a palpable gloom, and the wind seemed a tangible wall that was not broken through by strenuous effort, but that merely gave way before it, inch by inch, and sullenly. I would thrust my pole forward, brace, *run* the intervening steps to its rest, halt, take breath, and so on with a new struggle.

It was rough work, but the sense of solitude and uncertainty, of fighting the wild elements—the wild elements themselves in their first rigor, their fury newly wrought and unexpended—was more than ample pay.

Still, as I went my devious way up the final climb, the road and its guidance ending with the base of the cone, knowing not whether I was nearing my destination, or was *aimlessly* contending with difficulties, I was not sorry to hear a cheery voice call:

"What ho!—Comrade!"

"What ho!" called I in return, and with divers shouts and salutations heard with difficulty through the noise of the storm, my friendly seeker found me, and we trudged over the scanty space remaining with ease and good cheer.

We had alike climbed in the Sierras, and the Coast Ranges, and the Rocky Mountains, "but," said he, "never found I aught more forbidding and tiresome than the merciless harshness of this ragged granite, and the frightful impenetrability of this fog. I have been wandering for hours on the Crawford side, before reaching the summit, and when I heard that you intended coming up to-day, and that a lady had been seen on the lower ledges some time before the storm shut down, I thought, she will find this harder work than she has found higher climbs, and if she is half as lonely and blue as *I* felt before getting out of the beastly fog, she won't object to the word and the sight of a friendly human being."

Sight and word were welcome.

II.

As I went, that afternoon, over to the Signal-Service house, I wondered what one of the young fellows there would have given for a touch of human companionship through some dread days and nights that, to him, were filled with worse than solitude.

The cabin was small, yet too large to keep warm or dry; contracted, yet too extensive to grasp and hold even a show of comfort. The outer division filled with supplies, the centre devoted to stove and cooking necessities, the little room at the inner end crowded with the scientific apparatus, writing-table, bed, stove, living and working tools of two men. The carpet rotted to shreds, the paper and canvas hanging in festoons from the saturated walls, the windows abbreviated and opaque!—a dreary and inhospitable place in autumn mist and wind, a blot in a summer sunshine, what then must have been this shelter to two men, when, for seven months, it constituted to them the whole habitable world?

Alone on a mountain, and the mountain not approached even at its base through the bleak and furious winter; snow and sleet, wind and hail raging about them, the air dense, the storm around them oftentimes moving at the rate of a hundred and forty miles an hour; their sole link of communication with the living and thinking universe, a tiny thread of steel, constantly menaced, spite of its cable covering, by the savage blasts.

Even with the elasticity of youth and health, doubtless some weights clogged their spirits; what, then, must the one and the other have endured, as, in the midst of the wildest storm even this bleak solitude ever knew, with all possibility of succor or help annihilated, the one sank, step by step, through fever and delirium to death's repose, and the other, powerless to stay or to save, watched his comrade die, and then sat through days and nights in this sorrowful companionship!

When, through superhuman exertions, at last assistance came, to this lonely watcher it must have seemed like the opening of the tomb.

Since then, *three* gallant young fellows wait and serve science, sheltered by better and warmer quarters, perched on this inhospitable peak. I hope that nothing worse than health, content and happiness may come into their heroic work and lives.

"My view?"

I had no view.

As I sneezed and growled through the afternoon I bethought me of a fearful and wonderful woman arrayed in a purple velvet riding-habit, whom I had beheld on the apex of Washington, in the days of shoddy and '66, who hurried out of the Tip Top House, and into her saddle, exclaiming, with unconcealed and uncompromising disgust, "Well! what in the world people *do* climb all this way up this nasty mountain to get dinner for, when they can feed a great deal better down to one of the hotels, beats me!"

It beat me. If I hadn't come up these twenty-eight times for my dinner, and a precious bad one at that, for what had I come up? Certainly that was the extent of my gaining and getting when I *was* up.

But being down, after many asseverations of "no never"—finally modified to "well—hardly—ever" again will I go—I went; but this time in autumn, followed again and yet again by September sights, and tramps, and climbs that were present delights and memories for a life.

Moral! Stay away from the White Hills in summer, leave them then to the folks who know no better; yet thou, O friend! being wise and following wise instruction, will be sure of happiness if thy feet turn that way through golden time and weather.

III.

No White Hills. What of the Catskills, then?

For somebody else—if somebody else will, but for me—no.

Beautiful?

Very beautiful—a trifle misty.

Good for artists?

Yes; unfortunately I am not an artist.

And then I never see them without a shiver, and I like summer warmth with summer season.

Shiver of passing cold?

No. Of remembrance.

Once upon a time — time January night—I went my way to R—. The river was open, though the ice threatened, and the boat uttered lamentable wails as the great "chunks" jammed it.

Will it grow warmer? Colder? Close? Disperse? *What* will it do? queried I, prodded by anxious thought of the next night's work.

The next night was marked for New York, and a New York audience is one that having once faced with favor one is always eager to face again. 'Tis better than a cordial—warm, quick, responsive, helpful, the most thoroughly generous and friendly one the continent has to show.

Also a New York fee is by no means one to despise.

Alas! thought I, if *this* costs me *that*, duty will *not* be its own reward. I shall cry with vexation.

A night filled with wrathful voices of wind and storm, a leaden morning, frightfully cold spite of the struggling fire. "Thirty below," is the cheering response to my impatient and chattering inquiry.

"Boat running?"

"Oh, *no.*"

"Going to."

"Can't."

"Not even try ?"

"Not much! Couldn't cut through that ice if she was made of hatchets."

"How is any one to reach the train ?"

"Can't reach it."

"But if they must."

"Must will have to take a rest." A pause.

"One might drive across."

"No one mightn't."

"Why not ?"

"Would go to the bottom *di*rectly. There hain't no path been marked, and the ice will be oncertain, in spots and places. A horse would smash through in a jiffy where a man might go."

"One could walk across."

"Meaning yourself, miss ?"

"Of course."

"Much," with a grin. "A fellow as big as two of the biggest one there," indicating a group of boatmen round the bar-room fire, "would be blown over *like* a feather."

"Well, two of them, with a sled and me on it,

and piles of buffalo robes, and plenty of money in their pockets, wouldn't, then—would they?" say I.

A palaver follows, with a sequence of assent to the request insinuated.

Three miles across. No sun. A few spitting flakes frozen in the air. The wind through the gorge made by the high river banks howling like a wild beast eager to seize—seizing its prey. We were whirled round and round, upset, straightened, twisted over and over, righted—went on our way.

Three hours of mortal agony: that is enough to say. Men were watching us, ran down to the river bank, helped us up, stopped to expostulate with some people who *would* get into a sleigh, stopped to watch them off, and call a last warning, stopped to see them get twenty yards from shore, then one and all vanish, in an instant, never to rise again.

I was trotted to and fro on the platform by some friendly disposed boatmen, who mercifully kept me from the fire, and, still half frozen, was put aboard the train.

The train was late, and "kept on losing time"

all the way down. Two engines; but the tremendous head wind almost stayed us.

Had telegraphed. Audience waited. Reached depot at 8.30 P.M. Plunged into hack. Double fare. Gained the dear old dingy "Institute" at 9. Teeth chattering. Stomach chattering (no nourishment for thirteen hours). Fingers stiff. Feet like wooden clogs. Winter cold through and through me. Was there to talk about a theme — which theme was not myself — did not amplify on the day's miseries, but plunged into the subject advertised—in a word, kept my engagement with the public to the best of my ability—and was kept reminded of the fact through some weeks thereafter by means of divers physical telegraph wires.

And then?

Well, then, after the whole matter was accomplished,——, who has said a great many witty and good things, and a many more of bitter and unjust things to and about women, in one of her diatribes uses that night and the waiting audience as illustration of the assertion that women never know the value of time, and have no sense of honor concerning business engagements.

"Why," says she, "could she not have spent

less time on her dress, or have left her home in a neighboring city on an earlier train?"

Precisely.

Under the circumstances the question is both just and pertinent.

I *have* heard that somebody did once ask Mr. Beecher whether a man would have gone through that to have kept a lecture engagement, and that he did answer, "No; no man would have been such a fool." And was justified in the saying, only he should remember that the world, in reasonable fashion, demands of a woman that she do twice as much as a man to prove that she can equal him.

IV.

Not to the Catskills? Nor Niagara? Nor Saratoga? Nor the Lake country? Nor the Glens?

To none of these.

Suppose one halts for a summer's rest in Pennsylvania?

Pretty?

Pretty! I should say so. *There* is a place crowded with beauties. Had the people of *that* commonwealth one half the energy that is shown by New York and New England to draw and hold tourists, the State through summer, and far more through autumn glory, would be overrun.

If Mauch Chunk had some right-minded hotels on its near heights, it would be a hot-weather paradise. The Lehigh River winds past it, with innumerable devious turns through open country and mountain ridges that are as exceptional in broad beauty as are the glens and nooks, caves and waterfalls in miniature charm ; and there is the Switchback where one can have the delight of being pulled by stationary engines up one rise of six hundred feet in a length of twenty-two hundred, then another of five hundred feet in a length of two thousand, and then, taking the " back track," can return by gravity over some miles of travel, without engine and without obstruction, that will suggest the flight of a bird through the air.

The town itself seems as though it couldn't breathe very well from having its ribs jammed in ; as you enter it looks as though it has space for about an hundred houses ; but, terrace beyond terrace, the kitchen garden of one house trespassing on the front-door of another, the town holds five or six thousand souls.

And from this unique spot one can so easily slip

away to Wilkesbarre and the Wyoming Valley, which is the "happy valley"—happy in loveliness, lying under the face of mountains that are "delectable" beneath either a summer or a winter sky.

And there is the Cumberland Valley, framed in the delicious swells of the Blue Ridge, a delight to look upon, its beauty enhanced by the abounding prosperity everywhere made manifest in noble old houses, places exquisitely kept, barns as picturesque as they are liberal, fields that show food for a nation, and "cattle on a thousand hills."

Nobody looks poor nor suggests poverty.

The people, I should judge, are given generally to few excitements, few changes, and great tenacity of grip when they do seize upon an experience or an idea.

"I surmise Mr. John B. Gough is somewhat top-topical," commented a well-to-do native in my hearing, "lifted up by his great successes. I went to shake hands with him when he was here last week, and he actually did not know me, though I was introduced to and talked with him for some time after one of his lectures at the Academy of Music, in Philadelphia, five years ago."

That man ought to have made the acquaintance of another man who came to me at Altoona, with the reasonable request that I would tell him all the towns in the State.

"You are travelling all the time," said he, "and I suppose have gone up and down, and over and about every square inch of this State, and must know all of its towns by heart. Now I am a Pennsylvanian, and very proud of being such" (he evidently was not familiar with its representative, Col. Thomas Scott's private property, which private property the Pennsylvania legislature is popularly reported to be), "and I would like to become more familiar with my own State, and, if you please, I would like to call on you to-morrow, and secure some information in a friendly talk with you, and will, at the same time, jot down a list of the towns, together with any facts concerning them that may lie handy in your memory."

Let us not pause here. No. Lest he still lie in wait with his reasonable category, let us flee away, away, and, in response to the invitation given me long since by an enthusiastic soul, let us "rush to the arms of the Great West and swing out into Destiny."

V.

'Tis a wide swing.

Query :—*Where* shall one fall off?

In Minnesota? *Somewhere* in the region of the Upper Mississippi?

Comfort forbids.

All through its basin the summers are as much too hot as the winters are cold. Never went I there without finding pleasure in many things—among them the fact that my lot in life was not hedged by these boundaries. The air is so thin and clear, and holds so little moisture as to be an unobstructed medium for either heat or cold, and, as I there heard defined, they "boom" through it accordingly.

Suppose one drops down at Chicago? Agreed. Long enough, at least, to discover that there are fifty places of summer resort not half so delightful in June weather as this city.

So it seems to me.

But then Chicago is one of my weaknesses.

Still I think the open country will be better than the contraction of these walls, so we will "move on."

To California ? By way of Omaha and the U. P. ?"

I don't know.

To California went I ten years ago, and I wonder whether the memory will not be better than a fresh reality ?

From time to time, as one halts by the way, one can see Omaha grow and improve and beautify ; but has it the early charm ?

Coming into it now is like coming into San Francisco from the mountains or into New York from the surrounding creation. There is the cosmopolitan air, city and no mistake, that your born cockney and old campaigner alike delight in.

What hotels it has, and what *a* hotel, and what reasonable prices, and what capital restaurants and attractive shops—Paris ware and Indian ware jostling each other—and what wide, fine streets, and handsome houses, and enterprising papers, and what courteous editors, and, above all, what frank, friendly, active, wideawake people ! Omaha is a vital place. That is the long and the short of the matter, and the people who abide there are not content to simply *exist*. They are *alive*, and they are alive all through.

Still, it has lost something of the delight it held

for the "'Sixty-niners." Its "free and easy" air is quite gone since it has grown respectable and solidly prosperous.

That summer, people felt they had reached the jumping-off place, and acted accordingly. Heavy business men and staid matrons, grave doctors and learned lawyers, fashionable fine ladies, Congressional committees and committees' attendants, ran and drove to and fro, and "viewed the landscape o'er," with a sense of freedom and emancipation from restraint such as never blessed them before.

Now one goes through from Chicago to Council Bluffs across the bridge to Omaha, and so onward without incident; but *then*, every one, when fairly over the ferry and out of the big omnibuses, made for Cozzen's, and a bath, and a good supper, and a long delicious sunset and twilight time on the upper verandas, and a universal handshaking as one, and another, and another party drove up or came in; for somehow all of us who went over the first summer were acquainted, and everybody laughed and was happy, and congratulated everybody else on being able to see "all out-doors."

Also everybody put in a personal claim on the

giant enterprise that was to put us through. What was the use of the People building a Pacific Road if the People could not ride on it as they saw fit. The officers needed to be good-natured—with the rest of us—and they *were*.

3.57 P.M. ; train time out, 4 P.M.

"Is Miss D— aboard this car ?" calls the cheery voice of the efficient, genial, obliging, assistant superintendent of the " U. P.," Mr. Hoxie.

"Ay," is responded.

"Because," goes on the voice, "she has forgotten something——"

Anxious search for pocketbook and hand-bag. All right. Inquiring look fastened on the pleasant face.

"And I've brought it to her," holding up a "pass," and laughing as he comes forward.

A deprecating hand put out, a deprecating voice replies, "I never did travel on one of those things, and I never will."

"Not so fast," he says. "Reconsider. You are the *first* person who has been through here in the month since the road has been open who hasn't asked for a pass ; so we concluded you had demonstrated a right to it. There it is. It wouldn't be the handsome thing to go back on us."

So I take it, and shake his friendly hand, and thank him—and use my ticket just the same, and keep the pass as a trophy.

VI.

Presently I found myself, as before and since, both amused and disgusted by some English tourists wending their way westward—the sort of men who know very little at home and do not travel abroad for the purpose of adding to their stock of knowledge, landing at New York, looking neither to the right hand nor the left but streaking across lots to the buffalo country for the sole purpose of slaughter.

How many times have I heard the old settlers and hunters anathematize these bloodthirsty fellows who are destroying the magnificent creatures by thousands—for nothing save as a gratification to their own gory vanity, killing the grand brutes out of season when their dead bodies cannot be utilized, and in such numbers as certainly cannot be eaten. I remember, at Georgetown, Colorado, hearing one of these gawks boast that he had killed seventy-eight buffalo—the most of them young—and wondered why there was no law to clap an iron claw on him for his cruelty and wanton destruction.

'Tis a great shame that Congress does not interfere in behalf of these "wards of the nation." They, like their more troublesome friends the red men, will presently be all gone, and being gone, at least in their case, we shall hear lamentations and mourning, when neither mourning nor lamentations can restore them to their hunting grounds.

Concerning their chief tormentor—the style of Englishmen just noted—with his cockneyisms and insolence, his ignorance and rudeness, his sneers at every thing he sees, and his failure to see any thing, his eatings and drinkings—he and his *confrères* who cut across America *doing* and *appreciating* it, are about the best-hated people who travel.

Luckily—provided our English cousins care for our verdict, good or ill—they send us, as offset to this species of animal, the most entirely delightful companions one can meet on or off the road. Epitomes of thoroughness and genuineness. Perfectly bred, read and wed. Hearty and heartsome. With opinions of their *own*, and a readiness at all emergencies to "pull their pound."

Attributes not picked from every bush, let me tell you.

As to the *other* style—*Justice* all round! Out of the eastward bound train came a little fellow, by name—no matter about his name—and *American*, who fell upon me with vivacity and vociferousness. Two years before I had met him and his wife bound on a lengthy tour of the Pacific slope, she lecturing, he managing, and an adopted daughter singing, the whole made to "go" by a gift enterprise.

They were getting home from their trip, of which he proceeded to discourse to me. Had been in Nevada, Arizona, California, Oregon, Washington, Montana, Idaho, Wyoming. Travelled twelve thousand miles by their own conveyance, ten thousand by stage, and I don't know how far on horseback. A horrid little scrub who had no more eye for the beauties of nature than my shoestring. "A beastly country," he cried, when I said something about that marvellous Montana region, "a beastly country: WE *didn't take* $500 *in it!*"

VII.

Out of Omaha what was seen ten years ago is seen now, and will be seen, without essential change, when centuries have gone their rounds, until the elements themselves shall fuse, and matter resolve itself into fire and air.

What have I to say about it?

Very little.

How describe or do it justice?

I cannot. With Tom Hood, "I expressly decline to touch upon the scenery that hath been so often painted, not to say daubed already." There are some things of which it is better to be silent than to say too little—and this is of them.

If I were conscious that I could go west of the Missouri River but once in a lifetime I would not go at all, unless, indeed, the once could be for years.

And yet—no. *That* would not be satisfactory. One wants to go, and to come, and to go again. Not to *stay*.

Be sure of this though, my friend, if thou hast any love of freedom, and any longings after the sublimities, and any delight in space, and any passion for thy dear country, to grow constantly by what thy eye feeds upon, be sure if thou hast *once* gone thy way as far as the Rocky Mountains, each recurring season will find thy soul stirred within thee to see more and yet more of this amazing land that is *thine*.

Be sure if thou hast ever breathed the elixir of this air, and felt nerve and blood thrill within thee, thou wilt long for it, many and many a time thereafter, through all thy days, as one who having known *life*, can never be altogether satisfied with conditions of semi-death.

A word to thee, though, if thou dost go but once.

Do not make the mistake, as do almost all travellers, of confounding California and Nevada with Montana, Utah, Idaho, Colorado.

A *summer* trip to California is about as pleasant and wise a performance as to select August for the delights of New York.

Take California through the late winter, spring and *early* summer — 'tis Paradise. Take it through the middle and late summer, and early autumn, 'tis —— !"

Go to Caliornia in February and keep the country of the Wasatch, and Wind River, and Rocky Mountains for the return in summer time—and so be happy.

I bestow this information and warning without expectation of thanks, since it belongs to that least valued of gifts—advice unasked.

All the same, it is worth consideration.

For me and my first experiment : I left Omaha at the outset of summer weather, and saw it again at the fag end of autumn, twenty pounds lighter than when I turned my back on it, skin like a chip, juices dried in me, nerves tense, and brain on fire.

Any one who could go through the same amount of sight-seeing, and the same time and *weather* in California, without the same result, must either drink lager unlimited, or be blessed by *nature* with a happy stupidity.

And now, as I think of the ride, I reconsider my decision and advice, and say it is a good thing to go from New York to San Francisco, if you turn directly and go back from San Francisco to New York.

"This," said I, on our first day out, "this rolling prairie land of Nebraska is, after all, just like the rolling prairie land of Iowa," but by and by it began to take hold of me, and soon—all sign of human growth and enterprise vanished—its hold became a good firm grip that made itself felt.

Toward sundown, we met a freight train, moiling its way toward Omaha, the tender and tops of the car covered by an array of Pawnees, dirty, disreputable-looking creatures, all tatters, drunkenness and filth, who laughed and called, and waved their hands and rags at us as they went by.

It was an odd contrast! The steam wonder, cultured growth of brains and civilization, epitome of thought and mechanism, and these semi-human appearing beings carried about by it; and yet not stranger than to stand upon the rear platform, when night had shut down, and look through the flashes of lightning across the limitless spaces we were crossing, and recognize the anachronism of cars but no houses, and telegraph wires but no people.

I said I would *not* discourse of the scenery, and I won't. Still, having got over the plains, into the wild ragged country of the Black Hills, past the opening view of the far-away first range of the Rocky Mountains, through the gray, weird, ghostly Bitter Creek region--which must be wonderfully like Arabia Petrea—desert, yet mountainous and sublime — through the dreary sage-brush flats that follow, through the stately avenue of Weber Cañon, with the strange figures and giant sentries, and colossal faces looking down on you from castle wall and solitary tower, having gone through this, it is worth while telling how at

Uintah we took stage—not steam as now—for the city of Salt Lake.

And worth adding for the satisfaction and self-glorification of the "pioneers," and the discomfort of the comfort-seekers, that the first view of Salt Lake ought to be had from the back of a horse, or the top of a coach, and not from a car window.

It was at the close of a lovely day in June that I first saw the "City of the Saints," and, could I sell the memory, I should need to be steeped in poverty to the very lips ere I would part with it.

A great stretch of level plain; an inland sea of sapphire reflecting a sapphire sky; all about it range after range of stately mountains — their angles crossing and intersecting—glowing through the marvellously clear air, masses of amber, violet, and gold, whilst over all ranged diamond-bright the eternal walls of snow.

In the course of my wanderings I have seen a great many mountains, but for delicacy of outline, exquisite fineness of shape, clear cuttings of spires and peaks, I would back these ranges against the world. There are a plenty grander, more imposing, but these are so perfect in beauty, "the sense aches at them."

Mormonism ?

'Tis all so old a story there is no need of epitomizing, much less of amplifying it.

Die ?

Of course it will die. It can't stand contact of mines, and railroads, and the busy activity of travel and trade—the influx of the life outside.

Drop it. When it is dead, and the disgusting body buried quite out of sight, everybody will breathe the freer, and will marvel why such decay was ever permitted the semblance of life.

After a week's tarriance we got away from Salt Lake at four o'clock in the morning, and I could scarcely keep the tears from my eye as one after another the spires and peaks vanished, and the exquisite beauty of the view rested no longer in our vision, but in our memories alone.

May it rest there forever ! and may I yet again, with the eyes of the flesh, behold a full June moon shining through the crystal clear air, revealing yet softening, softening yet intensifying, the unspeakable loveliness of that scene.

I wonder, when spirits get out of the body, and have no trouble of locomotion, whether they will be as much interested to *see* as they were while caged. If they are so, they will have fine times careering through the air!

Certainly more comfortable ones than had we through the last two days of alkaline poison in the Humboldt Valley.

VIII.

Glad was I to abandon it at two o'clock on the second night for the stage at Reno that would take us to Virginia City.

It *did* take some of us, but it took not me.

As usual, I scrambled to my favorite perch on the driver's box, but was ordered down in language more explicit than elegant, and, as I insisted on a parley, and demanded cogent reasons for such descent, I found myself whirled through the air, and on my feet, with the marks of some brutal fingers on my arm, and a sensation within me, that, to speak mildly, was any thing but angelic.

Divers years ago a foolish driver of a Wells & Fargo coach, absorbed in converse with the lady who sat beside him, did allow his "leaders" to go their own way to the upsetting of the vehicle, and a *finale* of damaged heads and broken bones.

A reprimand to that driver? A warning to the others?

Not at all.

Wolf! wolf! you are always the wronged one.

Lamb, lamb, 'twas you that muddied the water! Lamb, lamb, *you* must be punished!

An order issued for the whole Pacific coast that no woman should be permitted to occupy the best seats of the coach—that is, the outside ones. All the same, I did; but not with *that* Jehu.

I took to my feet and marched along through the cool air, and looked across a country wild and beautiful, moonlight by which one could read revealing at the right the first line of the Sierras, white with snow.

Morning broke at half-past three, and I found an endless charm in the shifting and changing lights and colors the earth displayed as she received her king.

The grading was steep, but the road perfection, and it was an easy matter to keep either at the side or ahead of the chariot to the discomfiture and final despair of its driver, as he discovered that I would get over the twenty-two miles to Virginia City, and to a protest at the office, by my own methods of locomotion.

His orders were to be obeyed?

Of course; but he had no orders to show himself a brute if nature made him one, nor to indulge in assault and battery on inoffensive travellers, and I for one would not consent to such proceedings.

If any one wishes to see a road winding at sharp angles, and ever so many degrees round and round, and up a mountain through narrow defiles and across attenuated ledges, smooth and perfect as that on the Jersey sands when the tide has just gone out, let him drive from Reno to Virginia City, or, better, "drop down" from Virginia City to Reno.

No stint of money, or skill or labor here; and yet you feel on this road, as on some others round about, and at various points on the Union Pacific rails, that the Almighty was the great first engineer. These cañons, insignificant passage-ways between the vast piles of stone, are all that make the track of civilization possible.

Surely it would take long to weary one of these Nevada mountains. They are not ranges, but one universal upheaval, swells growing out of swells, mountains out of mountains—not peaked but rounded.

Bearing no growth of greenery, and yet not having the effect of rocks, because so smooth.

And then the lights! At sunsetting I have seen mountains of every shade and hue; a pink mountain, pink as a sea-shell, and as delicate in coloring; then a blue, and an amethyst, a purple, and amber, and red rose, crimson, pale green, ochre and brown, and even scarlet. Each mountain standing out clear and distinct; a mass of solid color, pink by green, ochre by purple, amethyst by blue, while afar—a hundred miles away—can be seen long lines and ranges of purple and blue so deep as to seem black, while over all is a sky without a cloud and without a flaw.

Perfection.

IX.

After Nevada prowlings we reached Truckee, on the "C. P.," at six in the morning, and fell in with the Angel of the Pass, Mr. Hoxie, of the "U. P.," aforementioned.

"Would you not like to cross the Sierras upon the engine?" inquired he thoughtfully.

"Rather," responded I, explicitly and inelegantly.

"Enough said. I'll *go* for the conductor;" and

he " went for" and fetched him, and so mounted us on the forward engine, and moved on his own beneficent way eastward.

Forward, for from Truckee over the next twenty miles the trains need two machines. Thus, then, mounted, the smoke, cinders, and dust all behind us, away we went, through scenery that 'tis but an aggravation to behold by such flying glimpses.

The ride would be a dream of paradise could it be taken by carriage and leisurely. Being what it is, in a little while we did not *see* at all, by reason of the prudent and protecting snow-sheds. Thirty miles of travel, cheerful as a protracted tunnel. Had the winter been upon us we might have had toward these stout timbers a feeling of gratitude ; as it was, we rejoiced over the loss of their society when we found " views" at various points through openings in roof and sides made by fires.

Twenty miles up from Truckee, we reached the summit, and from that point down, for seventy-eight miles, ran without steam. The engineer looked out of his little window, and held amicable converse, scarcely touching his lever save to stop and start the train ; the fireman went to sleep on his unused wood, the fire burned low. If the brakes give way—good-by to friends and home!

The grade is tremendous, often from 110 to 116 feet to the mile, and the wheels groan under the strain. For manifest reasons the distance is run slowly, safety is secured, but exhilaration is dampened.

Once out of the snow-sheds, the ride is one to take, and to enjoy, and to be still about, save to tell others to go and do likewise—forward, engine and all.

On the boat to 'Frisco I was too tired to look at *any thing*, so sat still, lived over the ride, and pitied the fate of a poor little dog whose acquaintance—and death we had made.

While the engines were shuddering down grade from the summit, I saw jump on to the track a pretty little dog, watched him with no special thought save that he would presently skip to one side—and there an end.

But no. He ran on, and by and by I spoke of him to the others. We then all watched, grew interested, absorbed, excited, leaned from the side of the engine, called, shouted, waved things in the air, and flung wood at random to draw his attention and induce him to jump aside, but the poor little fellow was probably too much frightened to heed or to understand our intent.

It was a sight to see him fly over the ties. Here and there his tiny forepaws would go through a cattle-guard, and as he stumbled the train would gain on him, but he would be off again! Several times we were so near as to lose sight of him, and then he would dart forward when we thought he was crushed.

It seemed like an embodiment of inexorable Fate — that vast thing going on and on, never halting, never hastening, and the poor little wretch with his panting, quivering being, trying a race for life with it. By and by he vanished. We had gone over him, and there was not a dry eye among us, even the engineer's held a tear — the little fellow was so plucky and had made such a game run for it!

Had we been on level ground the pace would have been slackened for him, but the grade was too heavy. Think of a bit of a dog beating an engine on a four-miles heat!

X.

What a good time everybody had in 'Frisco through that first "railroad summer." It was

Omaha repeated, only in the midst of comfort and elegance not to be rivalled anywhere. The hotel proprietors, the clerks, the waiters, keepers of shops and attendants, men and women at market-stalls and fruit-stalls and flower-stands, even the conductors of horse-cars, and cab-drivers looked at and smiled at and talked at the eastern folk as though they were long-lost brethren and sisters, happily found ; and the eastern folk—a good many of them—behaved as though they had reached a fresh "jumping-off place" beyond which was *nothing*, and they would act again "accordingly," and the rest of them enjoyed themselves regardless of cost and consequence.

For myself I never wearied of tramping about the streets, gawking at the people and the shops rich with the spoils of the world, and found ceaseless pleasure in running out of the city to any one of a score of lovely spots about it, coming back toward evening almost broiled, and plunging into coats and wraps as the fresh sea-fog blew inland, reaching a cosy room, calling for and sitting in front of an open fire that always gives companionship, and even in a barren hotel suggests *home*.

Or diving into the Chinese quarter, flattening

my face against their dingy little window panes, gazing into their dingy little shops at themselves, where, small trade going on at night, they pored over some book or paper, or in groups smoked and talked, or bent over their endless gambling with dominos, or peered into their opium-cellars, and at them stretched on mats, some beginning to smoke, some half stupefied, some quite still, having reached outward torpor and inward beatitude.

While I was at 'Frisco these celestials bestowed on me some hospitality that I like to remember.

They look like wooden images; dull-eyed and impassive-faced, with high monotonous voices, it is not strange they are accused of apathy of thought and feeling.

"There is nothing human about them," I heard repeated, till I grew tired of the iteration.

To begin with, I didn't believe it, and amply did they vindicate my faith in them.

In the course of the first public talk I made on the coast, I had somewhat to say of the Chinese problem, and said it.

This was a condemned theme. It was as "bad form" to discourse of the stoning to death of a Chinaman in California in 1869 as it could have been to protest anywhere in the States against the whipping to death of a negro previous to 1861.

The day before the speech was made, a steamer bringing a thousand of these " oppressed of the earth " (who should either be absolutely debarred our shores, or, reaching them, should for our own sake, receive the treatment *humanity* owes to humans) had entered the Golden Gate, and discharged its cargo to the tender mercies of American freemen.

What a reception !

I am an American with over-much national pride. What need to humiliate it by a detailed account of the entertainment ?

The reception being ended and crowner's quest held on four bruised and battered bodies of weak-souled creatures too feeble to breathe the strong air of freedom, verdict was returned, "Died of cause or causes unknown."

And the papers of the day, on the evening of which I held forth, one and all published the admirable decision of the twelve just men, without comment.

Naturally, I had a word to speak about the whole affair. To the great disgust of the people who had come to listen, with the expectation of being simply entertained, if not amused, the word spoken was—well, we will say *vigorous*.

And was simply the opinion of decent people everywhere, concerning the infamous treatment of the Chinese at the hands of ruffianly white men, and the yet more infamous silence of men of position and power, the professed superiors of these same ruffians.

To the dispassionate onlooker it may seem a trivial matter that a few of the myriads of " Chinese rats" shall die at an earlier day than the one upon which unaided nature would put a period to their wretched lives, yet even the *dispassionate* onlooker may well tremble when he duly weighs the effect of the sword-stroke upon the holder, not upon the victim.

It *may* be a small thing for some Chinamen to be wronged, and some other Chinamen to be slain, but it is a tremendous and awful thing—the unbridled and uncondemned spirit of brutal hate and murder in their American and Irish wrongers and slayers.

So say I now and here ; so said I in San Francisco to my first audience of friendly hearers.

Consternation was painted on every face, and an ominous silence fell.

Then what hissing!

At last a hand was lifted for silence. Silence ensued.

Said one human, within hearing, "She means to apologize;" said another, "She means to get off the stage, she's going to run away;" said a third, "She don't dare to face *this*."

Said the speaker to one and all, "My friends: You are not used to me. Never before had I the pleasure of facing you, and you, *apparently*, never before had the profit of listening to unpleasant truth. I will then tell you, so as to save time and trouble, that as I have endured a great deal of hissing, some stick and stone throwing, divers odorous eggings, and finally one or two revolver bullets, through Eastern political campaigns, I am not to be scared by a trifle of goose-breath in the West.

"Hiss as long as you please. The time makes no difference to me; but, on the whole, I think it would be more satisfactory for both of us, if you did it up in a lump. I will yield the time you want, providing that when you are through you will allow me to finish my time unmolested."

What a good-humored roar followed, and then what frank and hearty attention, as San Francisco, or some of the best of it, heard what the whole thinking world had been speaking about it, but from which it had hitherto been exempt.

XI.

"Gratitude an unknown quantity among the celestials."

Is it so?

Listen: the next day in my wanderings about shops I found myself among the choice of the Chinese, and straightway fell to investing in trinkets and curiosities, of which I found more than enough to beggar me.

The friend who was with me, and who acted as interpreter, Mr. Robert Swain, known and honored of all men—Mongolians included—in the city of San Francisco—him I made purse-bearer, and watched with interest the serious confabulations held between him and the owners of such goods and chattels as I saw fit to carry away.

I could make naught of their unmoved countenances, but his speaking face revealed—*something*—I knew not what.

"They always overcharge unwary travellers," had I been told many a time and oft. "He thinks he is helping me to the poorhouse, and is afflicting his soul in consequence," thought I to myself, as I went on with my gainings and gettings, leaving to him the task of "accounts."

Behold, when I reached home, I found to my chagrin that I had been making my "pick and choose" for *nothing*.

Not one cent of compensation had any of the "thievish Chinamen" consented to receive.

Of all the thousands in the city there were not a hundred English-reading ones, and of those I had seen not two could have understood a word of my uttering; yet, one and all, they had heard of and comprehended what I had said about them within four-and-twenty hours of the speaking, and, frugal as they are, repaid simple justice by lavish generosity.

Not content with this, to my great delight they decided me a dignitary and as such worthy a reception.

Think of it—a woman! and soulless! They are not tainted by that "vice of republics," when gratitude could so overcome both prejudice and religious belief.

Over Chi Lung's shop was a reception room (of Chi Lung, his shop, and the reception room cannot I speak in the present tense. They may still exist, or they may have one and all been translated to another sphere), a reception room for solemn high feasts and gatherings, and to this was I bidden, with some friends.

As a school for good manners I should not object to such visitation every day.

The seat on the right-hand side of entrance farthest from the door is the post of honor. To this was I conducted, mounted in state on the high-backed, curiously carved, and ungainly chair, and left to my own devices to behave well as I knew how—and so fell into disgrace!

The conversation flourished apace, since my entertainers all spoke some English, one of them being absolute master of it, and I never yet having lacked for words.

But alas for *feeding* etiquette! Presently came to me a sedate-looking servant carrying a huge box divided into compartments like a Christmas bonbonnier, crowded with nuts and sweetmeats.

What did I?

Looked at it, and picked out a half-dozen goodies from the half-dozen sections, of course, put them on the broad, flat arm of the chair that serves as a table, and watched the progress of the man and his box to my far-away next neighbor, who, to my amazement, took but *one* sugared poison.

—— always did love candy better than goodness, thought I. What induces *his* abstinence?

The box moved on to one, and another, and another—another, another, and one did but help herself and himself to a solitary sweet, till I gazed with horror at my pile, and whispered to my own means of vision, "Gray eye, greedy-gut," and thought I had need of being put back into pinafores with my nursery rhymes and manners.

"They are all old Californians," went on the inward monologue. "They all look a little horrified, even —— hasn't the courage to sign to me. Something's amiss! What?" and I, with lost appetite and hungry interest, watched the sedate servant cross to the *left*-hand side.

Did the first of my celestial hosts take one sweetmeat and then stop, I was lost! But no—

> "In he plunged boldly
> No matter how coldly"

the blood ran in his veins, gathered a handful to surpass my own, and heaped it on the table beside him.

I breathed again!—the more freely as I saw one and all follow suit.

"I haven't made a *faux pas*, after all," thought I.

Presently sedate servant, box, bonbons again appeared. My conscience was at ease, but involuntarily, as I stretched out my hand, I glanced across the room. Eight pairs of bright eyes were watching it, not anxiously; no, but closely. Eight breaths seemed suspended. *Seemed?* "Let us determine, take but a single temptation," said my internal monitor. I took but one.

Yes, it was so. *They* breathed again!

Afterward I learned that had I entertained them at *my* table, and had one of them seized upon a chicken and torn it with his fingers limb from limb, he would have done no greater violence to our code of good breeding than had I to theirs.

Query:—Would I have had the courageous courtesy to fall foul of a companion chicken, and rend it asunder to save the feelings of my guest, and make him quite at home?

We had brought us divers other delicacies in slow and stately following. Manifestly dyspepsia is not courted by these courteous Chinamen. By and by came some light wine in tall fragile glasses, that of themselves were enough to tempt an ascetic to drink.

For good and sufficient reasons being under a temporary vow of abstinence, I admired the exquisite glass, and the wine, like imprisoned sunshine, then pushed them to one side, went on with some earnest confab and gave no farther heed to the glass or its contents.

After a space came fresh glasses with fresh wine—they do not "fill" for you—and the first ones were carried away, and by and by, yet others.

At last I *realized*—I had seen without seeing, that the glasses of my friends had been carried away empty; my own, with those of my hosts had been carried away full.

Not a word said. Only it was supposable that I was of age to know what I wanted to eat, and *also* to drink. Offers of hospitality were made me. They no more thought of *insisting* on my drinking wine than they thought of cramming food down my throat.

Only what did not please their guest did not please them. What did, was right in their eyes and satisfactory to their palates, and we agreed on the tea that soon came in. Tea that was tea!

Had I been at a *civilized* table I would have been driven to the rudeness of obstinate-seeming denial by the rudeness of persistent request.

Will any one tell me why people who would shrink from the ill-breeding of *thrusting* food on one who neither needs nor wants it, account it civility to force drink on one who says to it *nay?*

For me, I think the Chinese are gentlemen. Let them so stand recorded.

XII.

Still I wish they could be induced to introduce somewhat more of cleanliness into their places of public resort.

One day, with some Chinese business men, gentlemen of elegance and culture, I went to the principal Joss-house, of which there were four in the city, and felt, when I came away, as though I stood in need of a succession of Turkish baths. Leaving the carriage we turned up a narrow dirty passage-way into a dirty courtyard, where were some dirty celestials chopping up a vile mess to cook for their dinners.

Another dirty passage-way followed ; another filthy courtyard, a door, a dirty entry, a dirty narrow stairway, a dirty narrow entry, a door— through which door, and after such tribulations of transit, you enter the Joss-house.

Room about thirty-three feet in length, nearly

square; dirty floor, bare; dirty windows at one end, bare; a table crossing the centre of the room, bare.; upon it some tinsel ornaments, not bare, but doubly grimed; ranged on the walls, objects that look like signboards covered with Chinese characters, gilded but dirty and tarnished; these and the tinsel ornaments and some tall sticks adorned with peacocks' feathers, gifts to the idol. An affair like a big umbrella, only rounder and deeper, a sort of giant tumbler, fine but dirty, to shelter the god when he takes his airings; hanging from the ceiling some colored glass lanterns to be used in his night promenades, a second table parallel with the other table, bearing braziers for burning incense, dishes holding lighted wicks floating in oil, and a little wooden horse, a foot high.

I asked, "What of the little horse? Why is he here?"

"*He* was a great warrior; lived sixteen hundred years ago. This is his horse."

Beyond the table against the wall *he* was perched. A sort of altar with drapery about it opened sufficiently to allow the appearance of a life-sized head and hand. This face had in it something noble and commanding—high cheek bones, large full eyes, red skin, darker than the Chinese complexion, full beard, the hand upraised with a gesture of authority, but no reverence whatever paid him by any one who approached.

"How do you call him?" I asked. "Who is he?"

"He was a great general."

"But what was his name."

"We do not know."

"When did he live?"

"We are not sure, but near sixteen hundred years ago."

"Do you worship him?"

"Oh, *no!*"

"Why then is his image here?"

"It represents to us his deeds."

"A symbol. You then worship his deeds."

"No, only as his deeds came out of his spirit."

"And his spirit—— ?"

"Is that of God. He did much for his people."

"Then you worship God."

"Yes, yes," they answered, with a vague look up and around, and an uncertain wave of the hand. "Yes, God."

In the dark and ill-smelling room was no priest and no ceremony.

Their great feast is at New Year time, and they come to the temple, if they so desire, on the first day of the month, or on any day through their holiday season of January, but there is no regular service at any time, and the Chinese who were with us, and some others who straggled in, showed not the slightest sign of reverence for any thing.

On one of the tables stands a wooden vase filled with "prayer-sticks," delicate strips of bamboo, with pointed heads, on which are stamped some characters and numbers.

A Chinaman prays, comes to the Joss-house, shakes up the vase, draws out a stick, reads the number, goes home and peruses the corresponding chapter in "the book," and his prayer is answered. He must interpret it as he best can.

XIII.

There are fifty places about San Francisco and its bay to interest and charm, and when one has driven, and tramped, and looked, and listened, till one is quite worn out, I know of no pleasanter twilight in which to sit and rest brain and body together, than the little Church of the "Mission Dolores," of which Bret Harte has sung in melodious verse.

Long and narrow, with its whitewashed walls, its statues of apostles, its pictured heads of saints and martyrs, madonnas and Christs, over all an air, not exactly of death, yet full of the repose of the tomb.

Its ancient lettering telling us that " this place is none other than the house of God, and the gate of heaven;" its holy-water founts yellow with age, the floor about them worn by the feet of those who hoped by this limpid clearness to wash away stains that soiled not the body but the soul; its old, old windows sunk in immense thicknesses of adobe walls; its antique doors, made wholly of glass, swung wide from their deep doorways, and through open door and window, revealings not of the restless life of a great city, but of a soft greenness that bends over a myriad of sleepers, lying silently enough beneath quaint carving, beauties of sorrowing art that age has not blemished, or simple cross or memorial stone.

Many of these sleepers, who were awake in a bygone time full of calm, were old when they shut their eyes on life—some dead full early. Did they, as those who follow them, prove the truth of the old Latin verdict:

"O vita, misero longa, felici brevis!"

and was it in sad or happy spirit they said, as we say now, O life ! long to the unhappy ; to the happy, brief.

XIV.

Surely never altogether unhappy to one who has before him the Yosemite, or, better still, carries its remembrance—a memory that can never die.

From San Francisco by boat to Stockton, from Stockton to Knight's Ferry, from Knight's Ferry to Chinese Camp, from Chinese Camp to Garrote (suggestive name in the mining regions), reaching supper and beds at ten of the evening after seventy-one miles of staging.

As to the dust absorbed during those seventy-one miles—justice cannot be done to it. It was *California* dust. What more can be said ? Not sand, not grit, nor any thing a traveller before knew by that name ; but *powder*, in which the horses' feet fall noiselessly, and which fills hair, eyes, nose, ears, throat, lungs, and skin, not only sifting through, but *dyeing* every garment worn.

At first I strove to be godly—I mean akin to godly—cleanly ; and so signally failed in the last as to overthrow all hope of the first. I worried, and shook, and brushed, and cleaned, and scoured till skin and temper were equally rasped and life a burthen, and finally decided to be *constitutionally* dirty and comfortable.

We were monuments of dust that night, and tired enough to sleep, even at Garrote, but quite ready for an early start the next morning, and impatient to reach Harden's Mills, twenty miles away, where we took horse for the Valley.

No baggage save hand-bags. Three of the party encased against wind and weather, unfashionable and picturesque; the fourth member of the organization arrayed in a soft felt hat, blue costume consisting of loose coat, skirt to the knee, Turkish trowsers, woollen stockings, and stout shoes. So armed and equipped we bestrode our beasts, and were away to the Yosemite, not, however, till we were joined by another party bound to the same destination, one of the ladies surveying *our* lady with disdain, and audibly desiring her companions to "look at that vulgar creature."

And the vulgar creature, from her safe and comfortable and *natural* seat, surveyed the wretched "ladies' horses," sore of back, lame of leg, beheld the girthing and tightening and fussing over the groaning and miserable creatures, the lift into the saddles, the ungainly bags of figures composed of half-long skirts and clumsy "waterproofs," the twisted bodies and uncomfortable attitudes—took a mental look ahead at the twelve hours' ride over rough and dangerous roads, smiled to herself, and thought, "look at those idiots."

Sensible and foolish, we started and rode hour after hour through solemn aisles of majestic trees till, toward the close of the afternoon, we reached open ground, where broke upon us the overture to the great harmony toward which we tended—a sight to take one's breath, yet merely the vestibule of the King's Temple beyond.

"Here," said the guide, "we begin the descent to the valley."

And we *descended*.

Mesdames, the critics, indulged in a good deal of screaming, slipped at divers points, sometimes voluntarily, sometimes involuntarily, from their horses, walked over the roughest places, summoned guides and masculine friends to lead their animals, to render help of voice and hand, embraced neck and mane of their four-legged servants, till the poor beasties having this misery added to their torturing girths must have almost smothered, and held on to saddle and pommel till hands, arms, and chests were strained to numbness.

And no wonder!

Said Cushing, my tall, long-limbed, bright-haired, wide-awake guide, who had bestrode every thing from a circus horse to a bucking Indian pony—said Cushing, after jerking over and tightening down for the twentieth time one of the one-sided leather abominations, "There ain't dust enough" (*gold* dust, innocent Eastern friends!) "lying round loose to hire me to ride on one of those things."

"Afraid of your neck?" said I.

"You bet," said he.

Through countless tribulations even the social martyrs reached the end of the seven-miles' *plunge*, and rode forward, with the Ishmaels of the party, into the Great Valley, the world's wonder, a sight for men and angels to gaze at with awe!

Before us, at the left as we entered, shutting in the view, stood "El Capitan," a perpendicular wall, no growth marring it, no jagged points thrust out from it, no waste nor *débris* at its base, rising clean and grand thirty-one hundred feet from a line already four thousand feet above the sea. Broad and strong at foot and summit, it gives, more than any other rock in the valley, a sense of solidity, power, massiveness.

Round the base of this we rode, rock after rock coming into sight, taking strange and airy and wonderful and sublime shapes, changing and changing again as we moved along and beheld them from different points of vision.

Through the valley we advanced for the first time through the solemn stillness of the night, the moonlight half revealing, half concealing the awful mountain majesties circling round and resting with chastened splendor upon a fall of water so white, so airy, so delicate as to seem the ghost of a torrent, dropping its length twenty-six hundred feet!

Tired as I was, aching from head to toe, I forgot I had a body as I gazed. Still, to confess to human weakness, I shed no tears when, at nine o'clock, we found at Hutching's ranche a comfortable supper, and beds that would certainly lull no sybarite to slumber, but were better than double action spring mattresses to our weary brains and limbs.

I know of no more hopeless task than the effort

to convey to another any apprehension of this marvel of nature's handiwork. The popular idea is that of a sort of magnificent *gulch*—two great walls of rock broken at their summits.

The *reality* is a valley eight miles in length, and from half a mile to a mile in width, a mountain stream rushing, white-crested, through its centre, great pines adorning it, and the freshest of grass covering the ground.

From this quiet greenness, level as a city avenue, with no gradual slope, these marvellous shapes abruptly rise in air, white, shining, clean of verdure, perfect in outlines, three, four, five thousand feet high; rocks like cathedral domes and castle towers, rocks pointed so sharply as to seem like needles, and rocks tapering off more softly and slowly to their heads.

These fine and grand, these penetratingly beautiful shapes, have been painted and copied and photographed till multitudes are familiar with their outline, but neither picture nor description can convey any hint of the height and depth, the greatness, the majesty of it all, and description added to picture, and picture studied, and then the eye used on the living presentment, all fail to enable you to grasp the marvellous whole.

You gaze and count, wonder and calculate, make your neck ache and your understanding crack, and you say "this is *two thousand*," or "this is *five thousand* feet high," or "this fall plunges down a thousand—twenty-six hundred feet," and you iterate and repeat till the words and figures bear no sense to your mind, and are but empty sounds.

There is nothing whereby to compare. The trees in the valley elsewhere would be marvels. There, standing at the base of one of these stupendous piles, they seem but common scanty growth, and this pile, among its neighbors, is simply a rock in the midst of rocks, and if you try to *compel* an understanding of the thing before you, you stretch and struggle till the brain feels bursting, and at last confess your impotency. You cannot grasp and take it in.

When we see from above, when the trammels and bounds of earthly calculation and human ability are thrown aside, we may comprehend Yosemite, but not now. It is the spiritual eyes alone that can behold with the *possessing* vision this god-like scene.

But, to a mere human, what days of delight does it afford and what memories to hold in trust!

I bethink me of one evening when we tramped past the lovely heads of the Three Graces, the stately strength of the Sentinel, and the solemn majesty of the Cathedral Pile to behold the sun-setting on one of the strangest " Bridal Veils" in the world.

Assuredly the spirit for which it was made must be "tall," and ought to be "young and fair," since itself is in length nine hundred and fifty feet.

Narrow at its top, and fanning out as it falls into lace-like mist and filmy gossamer spray. Here and there through its spider web the water gathers into arrow-heads drawing after them long spreading tails, and looking, as they shoot downward, like marvels from frost or fairy land.

It had rained through the afternoon, and as we stood at the foot of the fall, there were in full view four distinct bows spanning the valley from the North to the Half Dome, with sections of other bows flung about in lavish splendor. The fall itself was a dazzling mass of prismatic hues, the sky and air filled with rosy and amber light, till at last the glorious colors crept slowly up their shining ladder and left the fall to a gray pallor that was wraith-like and sad.

And of one morning when we rode over to Mirror Lake, lying outside the valley, on the placid surface of which the mountains around reappear with marvellous fidelity, not only in shape and coloring, but seemingly in the very texture of the rocks, till, as you gaze downward, you clap hand on head, and prospect for signs of feet, to decide the relative positions of each, and so make sure which is mountain and which shadow.

And of other and yet other days upon which we clambered up the white granite face of this or that giant, to look out at his comrades, and did not go astray, because we could not, in finding sights that would have repaid the expenditure of any amount of time and toil.

And of one supreme day when we mounted steed, rode away under the stately forest growth through the pass by the Half Dome, close to the side of the sparkling and plunging Merced River, till the trail grew so steep and narrow our animals could no further go, then, dismounting, took to our own feet and the companionship of stout walking-sticks up a most forbidding pathway that led us to the Vernal Fall.

A leap of three hundred and fifty feet, white as falling snow, glittering as gems, laughing and dancing down its wall of glacier-like rock, not grand, nor solemnizing, nor overwhelming, but just *perfection*—that is the Vernal Fall.

We dived into waterproof cases and clambered on. The mud ankle deep, the blinding spray beating against us like a heavy fall of rain, so past its base, then, dropping the unwieldy over-garments, scrambled by its side, up, up a ladder placed against the flat cheek of granite, then up, up, up another ladder, and so were at the top.

A broad smooth table of stone, at its outer edge a natural parapet, breast high, and shaped as though made with hands, over which one can lean and look for hours—not content with this I crawled to the point where the water plunged over the lip of the fall, thrust out my head, and tried to gaze my fill at the dazzling mass as it swept down and away. Below it the shining line of the river. The rocks of the valley in the near distance. Afar a world of mountains. Overhead a few fleecy clouds showing against a sky that was like polished turquoise.

After a space—oh, woeful falling off—we travelled onward to a charming spot, midway the head of the Vernal and the foot of the Nevada Falls, camped, ate our lunch—low be it spoken —with the appetite of wolves, then, rested and refurbished, went our way to the Cap of Liberty.

The mountain is exactly defined by its name. It is as perfect a Liberty Cap as though it were the great original, and the most beautiful object to be seen even here.

Standing solitary from its base, not a rock touching it nor even resting near, its face and sides white as purity, bare as penury and upright as truth, its back a slope dotted with timber that makes it possible of ascent, forty-eight hundred feet above the valley, and the valley four thousand feet above the sea.

None but Indians and a venturesome guide had hitherto ascended it, and at starting we were cheered by dismal forebodings and prognostications of defeat.

Well, we went up it. What else should we do ? A hard climb, a hot climb, a steep climb ; there were spaces where we had to take off our shoes and travel in stocking feet—gingerly at that, and there were places where my tall guide, having first " skinned up " perpendicular walls of rock, then flattened and bent down, did his best to dislocate two pairs of arms as he " yanked " me bodily to standing ground beside him, and there were shining shelving reaches, glittering and slippery as ice that we crawled over on hands and knees, and there were stretches of journey where we were parched for want of water, and there were rattlesnakes in abundance, two of which I killed with stick and claw, and was vastly inflated by the achievement, and finally there was the summit!

A fragmentary view of the valley on the one side; on the other the " Little Yosemite," at this distance almost rivalling in beauty its great name sake; two far off mountains, " Cloud's Rest" and the " Cathedral Peak," dwarfing by their majesty those near at hand; ranges and spurs of the Sierras with glittering heads, looming up across emerald spaces, here and there a point so blue as to show black, so steep and high as to be blown bare of snow, and close beside and above us, across the pallid brow of the " Half Dome," a thunder-storm swirling and raging, deafening reverberations sounding from peak to peak, lightning ripping the air with the sound of tearing cambric, electricity clawing at the gazer with small fiend-like talons, and at last calm and an effulgent light as the sun, dispersing all blots and blemishes, moved slowly and majestically to the west.

So absorbed were we as to lose thought of time. When at last we made the descent, struck across the intervening mile to the top of the Nevada Fall, gazed at its 700 feet of splendor, dropped down its side, and finally gained the parapet of the Vernal Fall, the air was no longer dusky but dense—it was not twilight, but night.

Certainly the ladder transit was wild enough, back foremost, hands and feet both in hard service, but that was *holiday* toil to the rest of the tramp!

The way was dark. The path was slippery, stones, and foot-deep mud making each step a danger; a wall of rock on the one hand, the wraith-like fall of hundreds of feet on the other, an abyss beneath; a thunderous roar filling the air, the spray and mist flying wild and white through the night. Below us Egyptian darkness, all about us sombre mountains, inaccessible heights, their tops thousands of feet away, peaks and points and towers and pinnacles and domes, shapes of beauty and shapes of grace, and shapes of majesty and power: these and these alone touched by the rising glory of the moon, and fairly glittering in its light.

All experiences have an end. At last we gained

our horses, plunged down the gloomy treacherous trail, and at midnight reached our temporary home.

Certainly we did very little climbing the next morning, but the next evening I mounted my pony and rode away alone for a farewell sunset.

Rain had been falling, a refreshing shower from a sunlit sky, and the air was full of a splendor of coloring that no pigment and canvas could reproduce. On one side the valley the rocks stood gray and drear; on the other rich crimson gave way to purple, purple to amethyst, amethyst to blue, blue to imperceptible shadings of delicate and exquisite hues, the effect being not that of tinted granite, but of a haze that left the outlines clearly defined, yet touched them with the softness of velvet. At the west, where the mountains close in, a scrap of sky looking like nothing so much as an enormous emerald.

I sat still on my pony till all the splendid phantasmagoria vanished, and the stone sentries stood brown, gray, black, deep shadows lining them, the gloom of night compassing them, watched by the solemn stillness of the stars; and the next morning we rode away from both daylight and starlight in the wonderful valley.

An all-day ride along the Maripose trail, to a

night's repose at " Clarke's ranche ;" a morning with the Big Trees and their majestic neighbors the firs and sugar-pines, each of these large enough to be elsewhere a world's wonder, good things to see, good things to remember — one must lift eye, and thought, and imagination to them even in memory—from these, fourteen miles of " deep sea-diving," an undeviating descent that puts knee-pans at a discount for some days thereafter, a ride ending at " White & Hatch's," where we were fed like kings and slept the sleep of the just.

A night coach-ride—the night void of moon and sights—suited not us who wanted to see *every* thing, so our last stage was made in a hired she-bang which took us to Stockton.

Truly a fine-looking turn-out was presented to view at four o'clock of the pleasant summer morning!

At least clean, whole, and unencumbered when we went into the valley, we turned away therefrom and set our faces toward civilization fit subjects for its chastening hand.

Capital horses, a spring waggon burdened with no luggage save paltry hand-bags, yet furnishing no superfluous room for its human freight

—a big canvas bag of moss, another of cones, manzanita sticks, and other sticks wrapped in shreds of garments, and tied together in unshapely bundles; clumsy pieces of big-tree bark; thumping pieces of big-tree wood; cones too precious to be trusted to the bag, held by their stems with questionable rags draped preservatively about them; long poles festooned with moss thrust out behind; presiding over all, four dirty, ragged, unshorn, unkempt, entirely contented tramps with their German driver, an epitome of horse lore and good-nature—a spectacle to provoke envy and horror.

Fortunately there were no critical eyes to gaze at us, and be shocked at the sight. With change of animals we rode that day eighty-five miles, and met not a soul. Everywhere yellow wheat fields dotted with oaks, but the country generally so lonely, so bare and parched as to give one a sense of desolation.

Yet surely never before was seeming desolation such real richness. We passed one wheat-field, unbroken by fence or stake, undivided save by the beds of two rivers (needing no division, since it was the partnership property of two men), fifty-seven miles in length!

Halted at a ferry thirty miles out of Stockton, and camped for the night under the light of the "Lone Star."

I have travelled, and I am not squeamish, and I've stopped at Western hotels, and *difficult* ones at that, but I confess to being appalled at this hostel.

A house without upper regions. The lower regions carpetless, furnitureless, save for a few benches about a central board in the dining-room; beds as abandoned by their latest occupants, and infested by "their legal inhabitants" (if length of possession gives right) in the sleeping cells; some phenomenally dirty wash-basins without accompaniment of water, soap or towels, in solitary possession of the *toilet apartment*, not another thing in the place but bushels of meal-like dust lying round or heaped up "promiscuous"—a species of furniture and ornamentation combined. At least it served to fill spaces that would else have been given over to absolute vacancy.

A big gaunt woman, mistress and maid, cooked us an atrociously bad supper, a big gaunt man, her husband, served it, a half dozen villainous looking drovers helped us eat it, after which, having failed to beg, borrow, or steal any clean linen for the beds, I made them up wrong side out, retired to my own den and slept on the floor —and avenged myself the next night at Frisco, by ringing my bell at intervals of twenty minutes, and having the entire procession of bell boys at the Cosmopolitan " roped in" to my service.

XV.

I would like to see the Geysers again—yes, and the " Big Red woods," and Santa Cruz, and Moore's Beach, and the pebbly beach of Pescedera, and Monterey,—and I would like to know if its human monument yet stands or has drooped to its original clay.

I went to Monterey to look at its old missions, and while there read in its little weekly paper of something more ancient than they — an Indian woman providing for herself and supporting her blind great-grandchild by working in the fields, who, as the Jesuit records of baptism showed, was one hundred and forty-two years old, and a little while thereafter I beheld her sitting by the roadside and paused for some confab with this voice of time.

Her brown skin, shrunken face, fiery black eyes, snow-white hair, cut square across the forehead and falling in a shower on her shoulders, with scarlet drapery flying in the wind, gave her an uncanny look that was a delightful change from the commonplace sameness of ordinary mortals.

When the Jesuit mission of 1779 was built she could scarcely have been called a *young* woman, yet she was one of its builders—carried stones and clay and timber with other Indian converts. These younger companions were dead and forgotten, and the Jesuits gone, the church a ruin, and the vast power of the priests a memory of the past, but the old woman lived, strong and vigorous. Does she live still?

And I would like to see Shasta and the Northern Range, and run down to Taho and Donner lakes, and while there I would like to be able to christen the latter afresh, if in wiping out its old name one could also erase the memory of its story. You know it?—how, years ago, one of the early emigrant trains was here belated. A delayed start, or too long tarriance by the way brought them to this spot, where they were overtaken by the first snows of the Sierras.

Part pushed on and reached Sacramento in safety, the others quarrelled and divided, moved forward only to turn back, the cattle strayed away, the counsels were diverse. They camped and waited—waited in vain for the succor that strove to reach, but could not find them through the intervening barriers of snow.

They ate all their supply of summer provisions, and as the dreary days dragged on could find nothing else to gnaw save themselves, and amongst themselves they cast lots for death.

A ghastly tale!

Forty-six of these wretches here perished in supremest agony and were at last found, some but bones, some partly devoured, some heroically dead of elected starvation.

Donner was the name of the leader of this party, and his name darkens the lake—pity that it has not one less fraught with awful associations, more in keeping with its own divine clearness and surpassing charm.

And I would like, turning from all this and more, to slip back along the rails to Cheyenne, clamber to the driver's box at six of the afternoon, and away for a twenty-two hours drive to Denver —and the mountains.

XVI.

But there is no coach now—no, and I am not at the western but the eastern end of the route.

Shall I go in *fact*, or only in *memory* over the last trip to the great Main Range, and the Arkansas Divide, and beyond?

Did I start from Philadelphia?

Yes, I did start from Philadelphia.

Alone?

No, with some very agreeable companions.

Will I tell any thing about Pennsylvania by the way?

No, that is too old a story; I did not look out for sights and sounds in that region.

All the same, one came to me, I remember, when the train stopped for supper at some little town near Wheeling.

Enter a specimen!

The oddest looking young fellow, who meandered about the new and handsome sleeping-coach, staring at it with wonder and awe, finally bringing up opposite my observing eyes, and untouched lunch, bobbing his head and pronouncing "evening."

"Good-evening, sir," I answered my friend, who reveled in red hair and a verdant countenance, big check trowsers and a "flopping" linen sack.

"I'm of a speculative turn," he continued, "I am. I like to see what I can. No offence.

I'm all right. See for yourself," and he fished a "pass" from the depths of a capacious pocket, and informed me he was a " school teacher *and* a local preacher—yes, and respected, I might venture to say *very much respected* too."

What could I do but bow and await further developments ?

" Sleeping-car, eh ?"

" Yes. P. P. Pullman *Palace* Sleeping Car," grinning to myself, as I invariably do each time I am called upon to repeat the snobbishly fine name.

" Heathenish !" protested he. " Couldn't they find some nice Christian name of a girl to call it for, without going back to that goddess—or whatever she was ?"

I gazed inquisitively.

" Oh I know, Pallas. I've read about her in the old Greek chaps. 'Tain't fair. *She's* had her day. She ought to get out for Mary, or Sue, or Jeannie, or something of that figure, hey ?"

" Right," I answered, " if you *were* right ; but you aren't. It isn't P-a-l-l-a-s, Pallas, but p-a-l-a-c-e, palace car."

" Oh ! that ! *Palace* is it ?" contemplating anew the superb upholstery, gorgeous carpet, and *sealed* windows. "Palace?" sniffing the air; "well it smells bad."

"So it does," I assented, "but that is the 'badge of all its kind.' 'Tis a family peculiarity. Railway coaches, as a rule, always smell bad. From much companionship the passengers grow so fond of their own air they can't bear to change it."

"For the land's sake! That so? My! What queer people;" and then with a gesture that might mean "enough of *human* affairs," my friend's interest in art revived. Gingerly feeling the rods and knobs he demanded—

"Silver?"

"So they say."

"*Solid* silver?"

"Oh, no," I answer, "only washed."

"Cheat!" he cried with manifest disgust. "Come from far?"

"Philadelphia."

"My! That so! Going far?"

"To Colorado."

"My-y! by yourself? Better take a companion."

"Have some," I say, pointing "at supper."

"Supper? sho! and left you here alone? Mebbe they're not sociable?"

I explained that *I* was not hungry.

He looked meditative, suddenly started, "Those grapes didn't grow round these parts I reckon ?" gazing at a little open basket of black Hamburgs and Malagas.

"No."

"Well, now, just for a curiosity, would you sell me a bunch of them ?" again fishing in the capacious receptacle, and bringing out a pocket-book. "I've got a *real* nice girl I go to see every Sunday night, and I'd like *well* to carry her such a thing as that. I always carry her something. *Will* you sell me a bunch now ?"

"No, I won't sell you one, but I will be happy to give you two," which I proceeded to do, and he was enchanted.

Just then up came the sleeping-car porter with a message concerning a cup of tea, had his answer and vanished. My friend remained with open lips.

"I say, *what* did that colored individual call you ?"

"Miss Dickinson."

"What's your whole name now ?"

"Anna Dickinson."

"My! That so! Why, you've got the same name as the big orator. Any relation ?"

"No."

"None?"

"None!" the disappointment in the queer good-natured face was too much for me—" since I am she—at least I am the only one of that name, big or little, who makes speeches."

"My! No! Why! Just let me sit down!" Which he did—heavily.

Rumination follows. Contemplation of grapes. Speech seemingly made to some inward ear—

"If I *could* keep them forever, I would, but grapes won't keep for ever?" looking inquiringly at me.

"No," I responded.

Face fell, brightened; hand fished again—out came a big clasp knife; face brilliant.

"Now, I tell you what! this is a big thing for me. Orators don't run round loose over my garden patch *every* day. Like enough it won't happen more'n once or twice in a life-time. Nobody at home'll believe where I got those grapes unless I have something to show for it—just let me slice off a little scrap of your hair."

A palaver ensued, and at last I pacified him with a card and an autograph, and the *whole* basket of grapes, and I hope he and his "girl" made a feast of them, and had half as ridiculously good a time over *them* as I had over *him*.

XVII.

The "companions" having come in, gazed after him curiously; then proceed to propound a question.

To which I—"Queer people? Met queer people in travelling? Of course. What other people *should* I meet? It is one of my firm convictions that the *only* people who travel are queer people, or worse.

"Of course with exceptions.

"Tell you about them? No, I won't tell you about them. I *never* talk in the cars."

"What! *never?*"

"Well——" no, I did *not* say it.

Don't I get tired of solitude? Sometimes, but solitude is better than prostration. There is no labor more fatiguing than that of yelling against the noise of the train and of straining every nerve of the head to hear—unless indeed it be to talk, under any condition, with the people who then and there assail you. If one has to use voice and brains and vital force in the evening, one can't bawl for the delectation—or reverse—of every one who seizes you with a "stand and deliver."

The reason why "professionals" prefer hotels to private hospitality? Precisely. No amount even of limitless fees can enable them to afford the latter.

Some hosts make a feast and bring together their friends and neighbors to see the animal feed, and that spoils the animal's appetite; and some collect a company to hear the lion roar—the fatigued lion preferring to stay in the corner and lick its paws, and getting abused accordingly; and some make great show of hospitality and expect the speaker—who of course is a clock wound up and always ready to *go*—to take out his board and lodging in talk, and that is an extravagant expenditure of strength and voice, soon ending in bankruptcy; and some are so considerate and kind and friendly as to suggest home-sickness, and afflict one with regret at parting.

No. The halting place for a traveller should be at a "traveller's home"—fine irony! Where one can eat and sleep and read and rest, and order and growl *ad libitum*, with none to molest nor make afraid.

I do bethink me though, that now and again I

have broken the rule of car silence to my content, or profit, or amusement, as the case may be.

I remember leaving ——— one morning very early—the early start of itself being a misery for the day ; and so sat huddled up in a corner of the seat, looking with a malevolent eye at whoso approached me with manifest intent of converse, when bag and wrap were lifted by a strong, white, shapely hand, and a clear voice just tinged with foreign richness said, "I will sit by Miss Anna Dickinson and talk with her for a while—at her good pleasure."

"Sit and talk by all means, my friend," said I ; and so a Sister of Charity took the seat beside me.

I confess myself astounded, for usually the Sisters are as reticent as the dead—and *seemingly* with as little interest as they in the everyday life of the world ; but this one had been through the hospitals of Great Britain—had wrought service in the wars of the Crimea, Italy, France, Germany, and had seen and heard with eye and ear, and with the understanding also.

She was an enthusiast, yet practical ; a devotee, yet full of interest in the things of time ; an ardent Catholic, yet a sympathizer with the movement for the social and intellectual advance of women.

Irish by nationality, forty in years, probably of gentle blood,—for she had the air of one born to command,—of dignified and noble countenance.

She asked me a thousand questions about myself and my work, and wondered I had not found the pathway to the mother church, "where all earnest souls belong. Ah, my sister, what a career, what work for you there."

"Where," she asked, and justly, "has the *Protestant* Church found or tried to make work, and place, and opportunity for the multitudes of women who have no vocation for marriage—what has been done for these has been done, largely at least, by those whom the church condemns."

Assuredly in this matter, the Church of Rome has shown the wisdom for which she has been famous, bestowing an inestimable blessing upon these myriads of women, and through these upon the world.

I never meet a Sister of Charity without wanting to stand in the gutter, if need be, for her to go by dry shod.

Knowing neither fear nor prejudice where poverty, contagion, disaster, death demand tending. Going with quick feet, and trained hands, and thoughtful brain, and tender heart, and pure soul to succor and help all who have need.

The nuns ? No.

They represent self-destruction.

The Sisters ? Yes.

They represent self-renunciation.

Two very different conditions.

The one buries all of her life that might think, feel, work for *her kind*, and expects through this grave to grasp heaven. The other buries all that would think, feel, work for *self* alone, strives to bring a breath of heaven to others, and finds it even here for herself.

May she keep it ! May the sun shine on her pathway, the hand of God rest tenderly on her, and lead her all her days !

So I mused when this one left me, and went her way to the accomplishment of some deed of help and mercy.

XVIII.

Hers had been a gentle influence and certainly I needed a quieting one for what was to come.

At L— I had to hear me the assembled wisdom of the State, and thought it made a very poor show. What wonder ! Three dollars a day !

The only men who will accept such compensation must be patriots of ye ancient style—which style is out of fashion at date—lewd fellows of the baser sort who take a little honestly for the sake of the chance at a dishonest much, or unclassified beings who make herculean efforts for the opportunity of strutting and fretting their little hour, and thereby gain a brief notoriety that to them seems immortality.

Why not ? when, one and all, we so constantly confound noise with fame.

One of these State Solons, a Senator cadaverous, and yet cabbagey of expression, did, on the following morning honor me by a call and his confidence.

Sinking into a corner of the sofa from whence he had arisen to bow stiffly, he besought at the outset the privilege of seeing me alone.

"Not here—oh, not here, where so many rude and careless eyes will gaze upon us, but alone, quite, quite alone."

As the hotel parlor sheltered, save ourselves, but two harmless looking women, I thought he might content himself with its extensive privacy, and endeavored to convert him to that opinion, but finally took compassion on his weakness and led the way to the wide deserted hall, where he, having first struck an attitude, proceeded to beseech me to promise eternal secrecy on the subject matter he was about to reveal, entreated me to be generous and just in my judgment, but, above all to be generous. "No, not so, to be just. Nay, rather, his human frailty *would* overcome him, to be generous. Do, do *not*, I implore, be severe. Read them! *Read* them! They are my best! Give me then your *candid* (?!) opinion." With which he clapped into my paralyzed hand a portfolio and key and straightway vanished.

With awe I inserted the key, opened and laid bare the secrets of this treasure house. Two manuscripts lay revealed. First, "The Rise, Sway, Decay, Fall of the Nations of Antiquity, with Thoughts, Moral and Æsthetic, thereon." Second, "The Republic of the New World. America the Hope of the Universe. Danger! What will save it! To arms! An Appeal to the Brains and the Hearts of the Sons of Columbia." Over one hundred pages given to *each* of these effusions.

With humility I confess I was not equal to the emergency. I fled for the first train, and, decamping, wrote him that his manuscripts required such serious consideration as to render it impossible for me to do them justice in the scant space of time that the exigencies of travel allowed. If he so desired I would give my valuable (?) opinion when I next came to L—, mentally writing a reservation that if L— saw me again while the legislature was in session I would deserve my fate.

That man was the worthy colleague of another member, who said to me, "I can't understand it! I have been making anti-capital-punishment speeches in a great many towns in some of our sister States, and of course in my own State, that have as much meat in them, *I* think, as any thing Beecher gets off, and are quite as thrilling as John B. Gough's temperance spouts, but they don't draw audiences!"

"Probably it is on account of the theme," I suggested.

"Well, yes," he assented, "that is about the conclusion *I* have come to. That—and the fact that I haven't the luck to be a woman. *They* draw well, whatever they talk about—out of curiosity."

"No doubt," I meekly responded. "Perhaps if you would have a brass band or something of that sort to liven up things you would draw better. People, you know, like to be amused."

"I'll take your proposition under advisement," he gravely answered, "though I'm not clear that people's light-mindedness ought to be countenanced and catered to even for worthy ends, by such teachers and leaders of public opinion as I. Still the matter is worthy consideration," and *he* bowed himself off, and I, as by a flash, bethought me of somebody I had seen in this same State some years before of whom this man was a legitimate successor.

A huge lumbering old fellow who tormented me through a long day's ride, having first introduced himself by the announcement that he "felt quite as if he were a relation, as he came from Pennsylvania, and his first wife's name—I've got my fourth now—was Nickerson."

Which self-presentation being accomplished he mumbled and maundered on, at intervals, through the next half dozen hours, some of his talk being distinguishable and some not, till at last I heard, "I was in the Pennsylvania legislature more than thirty years ago with Thaddeus Stevens"

"Ah!" I said, "Thaddeus Stevens has been in public life a long time—a great many years."

"Yes," answered he, "a long time. True enough. I and Thaddeus Stevens have been in public life a long time."

After which silence was manifestly in order.

Only, as after all these years I tell the foolish story, there comes before me a picture of the old, sad, furrowed, hollow-eyed, granite face of the "leader of the House," as it used to show forth through stormy scenes in desperate days that tried men's souls, and I hope, with all my heart, that when the dark waters close round us again there may be found such another head and hand at the helm.

The effect upon me of the oak that had served as support for the "Nickerson" vine, had been to put me so askew as to make me more than grateful to a curiosity who came into my way just as I reached my destination, for the opportunity he gave me to laugh.

A great hulking fellow, cased in a fur overcoat and fur gloves, blue overalls and a coon-skin cap, the tail dangling down his back, marched up to me in the waiting-room.

"Hey! I say! By the name of Dickinson?" putting out his mighty paw.

I confess it.

"Give us a shake. Proud to make *your* acquaintance. Heard on ye for a powerful long while. Came *a* long way to see you. Give us another shake."

Shake No. 2 gone through with.

"What's *your* name, my friend?"

"*My* name? Oh *my* name ain't no account. You wouldn't know it anyway. Where's the use? Ye don't know me nohow. Nothing to speak of. Teacher by trade."

At which I stood open-mouthed and watched him, coon-skin cap, and all, vanish away, overwhelmed by such professional modesty.

And consoled myself divers times the next day in the midst of a deal of discomfort by a fresh laugh at the thought of him.

And needed it.

The day was one of the "easy" seasons, of which a busy L.L.'s life is full.

"Such a delightful time to be sure you must have, running about the country with nothing to do but travel and be amused, and talk when evening comes."

Just so!

Left —----— before daylight, breakfastless, since

I have not the stomach of an ostrich. At noon changed cars at —— where was dinner.

Found a room with lavender colored walls picked out in deep maroon lines, green shades at the windows and bright blue ones over the doors, checked red and gray table-cloth (low be it spoken, filthy), napkins—none. The dishes—plenty of them—pitched on to the table, and looking as though they had engaged in a free fight after they got there. Not a whole piece of crockery to be discerned. The food, hot bread, cold bread, steak, ham, mutton chops, potatoes, eggs, milk, toast, stewed tomatoes, stewed peaches, pickles, cake, pie, recklessly massed together. All of them that *could* be fried in fat pork *fried* in fat pork, and one and all cold and disgusting together.

Luckily I did not see the kitchen till *after* I had eaten my bit of bread and drank my cup of coffee. Coffee? " Waiter, if this be coffee bring me tea, and if it's tea let me have coffee !" Otherwise I should certainly have fasted. New food and old, clean things and dirty things, dogs, cats, greasy hands, combs, cooking utensils, dish towels and soiled clothes mingled in wild confusion and disorder dire.

If the half were told of divers R. R. Eating

Houses, the chronicler would do well to absent himself therefrom for the future, lest, having escaped the perils of the table, a more violent though less suffering death should befall him.

From this feast to the poisonous cars. Rumble, jumble, jolt, jolt, jolt. Something the matter with the engine. Limp, limp to the Junction of other road. Three hours late. Train gone. Hunted up the superintendent of other road. Had a small palaver, handed over $100 and got my "special," but had to wait for it.

Waited for it in a queer place at the depot in which the railroad employees eat and lodge, a huge long room with a ceiling of rafters so low that I could stretch my hand to it, a dingy floor, dingy walls, opaque windows, men sooty and grimy crowding the tables, but the whole thing made picturesque and even home-like by an enormous open fire of soft coal sending long flickering waves of light through the gathering shadows of evening.

I was almost starved, but had to let imagination feed me. There was great abundance of food, but the "fry," and the "pork," and the rest of it, were too much for me.

The room and its occupants, though, made a picture to remember, as I turned from it, clambered on to my "special," and went away.

I sat in solemn state on the engineer's green leather cushion, feet dangling, furnace fire scorching one cheek, fresh evening air chilling the other, and took in the splendors of a lurid sunset while meditating upon the weakness and folly of poor human nature that will so constantly need control.

"Be thy own master."

Easily said.

Again and yet again have I lived through the same experience as that of this ride. An engineer without arbitrary orders or train time to obey, a good start followed by a run at such furious speed as to shake the miserable traveller to a jelly. A "hot box," a long delay, a limping termination.

All's well that end's well. We ran into —— at eight o'clock, and the engineer, per agreement, blew blasts that would have roused the seven sleepers to let the audience know ye speaker had arrived.

The audience was worth talking to—a compensation for the ills of the day. As to the association——

After having spent fifteen hours of travel and one hundred and fifteen dollars to keep my engagement, and spoken to a crowded house, the members of the aforesaid modestly suggested that I take half my fee.

"For why?"

"Oh, we thought there was no doubt you would be delighted to contribute to the excellent cause for which this course is given—a new organ for the First Presbyterian Church."

Seeing that I had no personal interest in that special denomination, and never had nor never will enjoy or suffer by means of the desired organ in that particular church, I respectfully declined impoverishing myself in its service, and have—*sans doubt*—left behind me the name of a greedy and avaricious woman.

XIX.

Some time I would like to free my mind upon this matter.

There is not a reasonably successful speaker in the country who is not put through a highway process till he or she would be justified in growing suspicious at the very sight of a "treasurer."

"Two hundred dollars a night. Three hundred and sixty-five nights in the year. No expense of travel. Feed on the air. Not a solitary soul in the whole world with any claims. What a source to draw from!"

That, I fancy, is the method of calculation.

If it were *true*, what then?

The "course" is given for the benefit of a free reading room, a library, a hospital; to refurnish the minister's study, to carpet the church aisles, to get new cushions for the pews, to put a spire on this church, or a steeple on that, to raise funds for a public-school piano; for a local charity, for any one of fifty different "causes" that ought to be supported *at home*. And a man who will not give ten cents to what is to benefit himself or his, directly or indirectly, will demand of an absolute stranger ten, twenty, fifty, an hundred dollars with an air of virtuous command that would seem to indicate a clear conscience and sense of duty well done.

Curious how many of Hood's hat-bearers you find. "Charity's a private concern" (say they), "and what I give is nothing to nobody."

For myself, I confess to a preference for being my own almoner.

Which reminds me of how quick people are to bring the charge of stinginess against "professionals" when they are known to have said "no."

A word in behalf of all. My experience has doubtless been the counterpart of others, and had I the revenue of a million with heart to distribute it all, instead of being a hard-working drudge, I would be beggared each year ere the year is half done.

Here is a letter—one of hundreds—asking me to take the mortgage on a farm, and here one to lift the like on another. Here one from an author to publish his book, since "the trade fights shy of it," and here one to free a milliner's stock covered by debt; here one to pay old college bills, and here one to furnish the wherewithal to keep free of new ones, and here is one from a young woman, wife of an invalid husband, who has gone from friends and home in the east to find "easy pickings" at the west.

(Will people *never* learn that if they can't *live* in the East, they will die a thousand deaths in the West. The West is for neither the lame nor the lazy. It takes twice the stuff in man or woman to get through there that it does to make a very decent sort of success over smoother and quieter lines "at home.")

This one doesn't know any thing about stock-raising or nurseries, but supposes that animals and trees grow as God ordains, and always to perfection. She thinks if I "would buy her two thousand trees to set out, and three thousand sheep," she could "manage them very well, and is sure she could make a good income from them in time. Husband is sure of it too." Though as they are twenty miles from a post town, and a hundred miles from the railroad, and are they two and no more, to me the outlook for future gain looks dubious.

I tell her so, and try to suggest a plan that seems to hold some real help, and madame, in her next letter, "forgives" me.

Truly in these masses of letters there is food for thought, texts for many sermons, matter for scalding tears. For God's sake, why don't fathers and mothers see to it that their sons and daughters are alike trained to methods of self-support!

XX.

I think my ponderings on the whole matter, association, letters, and all, were rendered somewhat more severe by reason of being made the next day, while undergoing the process of churning on the Illinois Central Road, which road always raises within me the question as to why it has any rolling stock left to be destroyed, and any humans to be ended. Fortunately it was carrying me to a Chicago audience, with Sunday to spare for Robert Collyer. Compensation in that!

What a wholesome, friendly, inspiring audience it is. One that understands, what so few people ever dream of, that the audience has almost as much to do with the entertainment as has the entertainer.

It is as though you looked at *one* person, and that person looked back stonily, indifferently, sleepily, repellingly, not at all, or with asking eye, eager color, answering face. When the audience *responds*—not necessarily by hand or voice, as well as *listens*—everybody has a good time.

For me, I have faced a crowd ready to talk, full of enthusiasm, well and strong, and in ten minutes have grown so tired I could scarce stand; and I have crawled off the cars after a twenty-hours' ride, shaken to a jelly, banged black and blue, asphyxiated with coal gas and the perfume of burnt iron and dirty humanity, and been spirited to the hall without rest, food, or a clean face, so tired that I wanted to prop against some convenient table or wall, and have felt, long before I finished, as though I could *never* be sick nor weary, nor disgusted, and having ended wanted to begin and do it all over again.

Some audiences are stone. You strike against them and rebound—angered by their hardness. Some are sponge—absorb, and absorb, and absorb, and give *nothing* back, till you feel as though you had enjoyed six hours of the Turkish bath and then been put under an exhausted receiver; and some are like champagne, or vigorous tea, or clear cognac, or aggressive coffee, or whatever it may be that the most quickly and enchantingly stimulates *your* brain and nerves.

That is Chicago.

And yet I wonder if even a Chicago or New York audience could fill that bill if it were put into a gloomy room. Darkness deadens. Light is life.

One reason why so many preachers *prose* to dull congregations, and why so many actors and singers and speakers do their best endeavor and fail is because, in so many cases, they are entombed in dingy caverns, filled with the air of a tomb.

I bethink me of a certain delightful audience, well bred and well read, that I used to see gasp and agonize—gasping and agonizing with them, in whose behalf I finally ventured a protest.

A low ceiling, a raging furnace, and flaring gas jets devouring what little oxygen filtered in through crevice or opened door—no "means of ventilation" save the windows opening at the back of the unfortunate crowd in the gallery.

Beseeching a mouthful of fresh air, these were opened, the rain and night wind driving in on the heads and shoulders of a hundred or so of unhappy victims, who shivered, drew closer wraps and cloaks, sneezed now and then, and coughed at intervals.

By and by divers hands were stretched forth, and the windows, with pauses, and inch by inch, reached the closing line.

More sizzling, followed by a fresh protest, ending in a duplicate experience; a delicious bit of coolness, speedily vanishing before fear of its consequences. Delicious to the platform and the floor—direful to the gallery. Protests manifold. The sequence of the speech being sadly marred by an occasional cry of "hands off," or language to that effect from the simmering speaker, who finally lost her temper and proclaimed "this is a horrible hall."

"*Horrible Hall!*" cried an indignant voice, while a red-faced and perspiring man rose to view.

"*Horrible Hall!* This is *my* hall, and I should like to know *what* you mean by calling it such a name."

"Because the name defines it," answered the irate speaker, nowise terrified, since she was planted "on the vantage ground of truth." "It is a death-trap. Fresh air is as essential to life as a pair of lungs. This is a grave—without ventilators."

"No ventilators! *What* do you call *those?*" pointing his cane at what looked like an unbroken expanse of smooth ceiling, and wildly waving it toward the four corners. "*What* do you call *those?*"

"Those?" queried the speaker. "I call *that* a ceiling.

"*In* the ceiling," shouted he.

"I see *nothing* in the ceiling," answered she.

"There, and there," he repeated. "Can't you see?"

"Where, and where?" asked she, making a telescope of her left hand. "No, I can't see. Permit me," stooping to one of the smiling ladies upon the front bench, and taking her opera-glass.

"There," came in a gasp from the fiery mouth of the now purple countenance, "*and* there, *and* there, and *there!*" the cane once more cutting lively angles toward the four corners, in which four corners could be dimly descried infinitesimal openings.

"Oh," said the enlightened speaker, peering through the borrowed glass, "I beg your pardon. Did you mean those gimlet holes."

"Ga-ga-gim-let holes!" stammered the angry tongue—it *isn't* soothing to rasped sensibilities to be laughed at by a thousand voices—"ga-ga-gim-let holes? They are *ventilators!*"

"Into what do they open?" blandly asked.

"Why—why, into a loft."

"And *what* may be above the loft—by chance?"

"A double action, patent waterproof, air-tight roof," bawled a smart boy from the gallery, whereat the audience roared, the defender of his property collapsed, or was dragged down by some judicious friend, and the evening went on to its *melting* close.

"The Lord save her husband, if she ever has one," she heard remark the irate and as yet unbleached proprietor, as she was edging her way on the "secretary's" arm slowly down the stairway.

"Amen," answered she, anxious to respond to

friendly wishes, "and may he be mercifully disposed toward your wife.

But the next year I found the roof with a hole punched in it, and divers ventilating tubes inserted in ceiling and walls "to the great comfort of everybody," said the proprietor, who, at the close of the evening, came to shake hands and to present his comely wife.

"I dare presume," he added, "that you ain't given much to soft-sawder, but I like your sense."

Plenty of air to send clear blood to the brain, plenty of light to stimulate—more of both, good friends, in houses, public and private, would be a blessing the delights of which and the gain of which are past computing.

XXI.

More than once the struggle for it has given me a deal of fun. Speeding over the Michigan Central one of the beings who must express himself or die, having watched me fume over my window till I had at last conquered the catch and secured a mouthful of fresh air, abandoned his seat on the other side the car, crossed and planted himself in front of me and the partially opened sash.

Presently he stirred, shrugged his shoulders,

turned up his coat-collar, and remarked, "It's chilly."

As the announcement was apparently made to creation generally, I felt no call to respond.

Dissatisfied at the silence he faced round and inquired,

"Would you like to have me shut that window?"

"No," said I, "I wouldn't."

For a space, silence.

"Did you want that window open?"

"I did," responded I, "and I do."

"'Tain't so warm over here as it is by the stove."

A pause.

"I said 'twan't so warm here as over to the stove where I was a sitting. You'd just better let me shove that down," persuasively, and stretching out a brawny hand.

"No."

"But I tell you the cold comes in lively," surveying the crack, half filled by the magazine stuffed into it, leaving open a mere mousehole. "I'm not as comfortable here as I was over by the stove."

"Why don't you go back then?" I charitably

suggested. "It wasn't necessary for you to come here, to begin with."

Another pause. A fresh charge.

"I say, ain't you cold?"

"No."

"Ain't you afraid of *taking* cold?"

"No."

"You haven't got any thing the matter with your lungs, have you?"

"No."

"Throat all right?"

"Yes."

A cessation of hostilities. Truce soon broken.

"I say *hadn't* you better let me put down that window?"

"No."

A breathing space, a vigorous hitch to the fur coat-collar, a longing look toward the fiery dragon of iron and coal.

"*And* you ain't afraid?"

"*No!*"

"H-h-h'm—*you* call *yourself* strong-minded, now don't you?"

"I would be sorry to call myself weak-minded."

"Speak. Don't you?"

"Yes."

" Make lectures ?"

" Yes."

" Get paid pretty well ?"

" Yes."

" Ever talk any ?"

" Yes."

" You don't say ! D'ye mind telling a fellow whether you ever speak mor'n one word at a time ?"

" That depends on circumstances," judicially pronounced. " At present I prefer not to talk at all."

At which he stared, pondered, looked at me, at the air-hole, rubbed his side-whisker, pondered again for enlightenment—*got* it.

" Meaning me ? Oh, you needn't apologize. I can take a hint as well as another fellow. I never put in where I ain't wanted, not if I know it. No. . . . Where might you hang out your shingle ?——

" I said where might your home be ?"

" Philadelphia."

" Philadelphia ? You don't see much of it, I reckon ?"

" No."

" Old folks living ?"

Silence.

"I said I hoped your pa was lively yet?" insinuatingly.

"No."

"You don't mean to say he's dead?"

A nod—in despair.

"Sho! Well! It's natural. People *do* die. Ma to home?"

"Yes."

"Ever travel round with you?"

"No."

"Never? And she ain't afraid to have you travel round alone? No? I reckon, then, you're a chip of the old block. Got snap to her, has she?"

I am too busy about the much discussed window to make reply.

"*I asked* whether your ma was like *you?* Has she got *go* to her?"

I am not yet done with the window and my dumbness.

"Well, we'll let the old lady drop. You don't like my talking about her, I reckon—from the color of your face. Got a temper, haven't you?"

"Yes."

"I thought so. Get it from your pa or ma?"

"Got it from being compelled to see and hear such people as you," I defined.

More rumination, side whisker again rubbed, situation faced boldly.

"Brothers and sisters like you? Maybe you haven't any. How many brothers and sisters might you have?"

"I *might* have fifty," growl I, "but I haven't."

"No?—*Lost some?*"

A relapse again into a silence fast verging on imbecility.

"Don't like to talk about your family mebbe. Some people don't. *I* don't mind. Leave talk about my folks as not. Got any objection to my asking how old you are?"

"None in the world."

A new and prolonged pause.

"You haven't told me."

"What?"

"How old you are?"

"You haven't asked me."

More meditation. This time resulting in *no* enlightenment.

"I did, but I don't mind asking you over again. How old *are* you?"

"Old enough to mind my own business, and to

tell other people to mind theirs. You really will do me a favor, my friend, by asking me no more questions."

The Irrepressible seemingly settled into a profound reverie, and I thought my purgatory was ended. Vain thought. He came up to the next round, smiling.

"Lecturing's your trade, ain't it? You make your bread and butter by it, don't you?"

My tired head nodded what served for an assent.

"Well now, all's grist that comes to your mill then? One fellow's stamps are's good as another's, hey?"

I am forced to admit it.

"Well now," growing emphatic and dragging out some greasy looking bills and currency, "look here. You'll never lecture in our town. It's too derned small. But *I'd* like to hear what you *can* do when your steam's up. I thought I'd get a free blow out, but I reckon you weren't born yesterday — got your eye-teeth cut. There's a dollar, 'll that pay you for a good square talk and all the fixens?"

I make it manifest to him that it *won't*, and hold my peace once more.

"What! not for a dollar? Well, then, it's

pretty steep, but I don't mind just for once going *two* dollars."

Not even for two dollars can I be wound up and made to go, and *his* forbearance is exhausted.

"You don't mind my telling you that I think you're pretty considerably much on the make? I never *did* see your beat. You won't be sociable, and you won't make a square trade! You're not the woman for *my* stamps," putting back his unwashed currency. "I wouldn't talk to you if—well, I'd as lief talk to a stone wall. Perhaps you'd like your own company?"

And as I did not contradict him, he gathered himself up, overcoat and all, and replanted himself for a slow roast by the fiery dragon of a stove.

But, evidently, bore me no malice, for, getting out at a lumber town, in the woods, he paused and said, "If you ever SHOULD speak anywhere round, I'll come to hear you."

XXII.

He being gone, before I could relapse into my usual condition of stony silence, enter another specimen.

This one came in from the smoking car, and peering about with a pair of small sharp eyes set too close together to commend their owner, presently spied me, and posting to the seat vacated by my lumber friend, proceeded, not to draw from but to bestow upon me.

"I heard you last night, Annie," he remarked, by way of an easy and friendly opening, " at ——. I don't live there. I happened in. Yes," he repeated, "I *happened* into the lecture," as though he were fearful I would be *too* inflated at his voluntarily seeking the show, and must tell me how it fell by chance.

I appreciated his consideration and awaited further developments.

"Yes," he reiterated, to make sure I fully understood him, "I went to hear you, and I must say, on the whole, I was agreeably disappointed. I didn't believe a woman *could* speak so well."

After a pause to give due weight to the announcement:

"I'm a doctor."

In spite of the weighty information, I was still able to maintain an upright position and gaze at him unfalteringly.

A half-dozen men who had changed their seats so as to be at close quarters, were sitting about very still, with a "weather eye" fixed on us, and one ear set at an alert angle to catch whatever might be said, as is the fashion of your true Western American when any thing is " going on," ready to listen or to strike in, if occasion offers, on either side, impartially.

" No," he went on, raising his voice and looking toward the conference meeting, " I liked to hear you well enough. You're smart. There's no denying *that*, but I don't like your sentiments. I think too highly of the sex—I'm a lady's man *myself*—to have them turned out to shoe horses, and build roads, and be blacksmiths and teamsters, the way you want 'em to be. I suppose you'd like 'em to wear trowsers, and chew," rolling his quid, and spitting an emphasis, " and drink, and swear, and go the whole figure generally, wouldn't you ?"

" Oh no, my friend," answered I, being thus appealed to. " I'd like you," surveying his little head and his big body, " and such men *as* you, to turn out and shoe the horses, and mend the roads, and be blacksmiths and teamsters, and leave vacant the places you are not *filling*, as doctors, or ministers, or lawyers, for the same number of intelligent, needy, wideawake young women, and *you* could cling, unmolested, to your congenial pastimes of chewing, and drinking, and swearing, to the end of your respective chapters."

He didn't like the suggestion. In fact, I have often noticed that opinions in regard to the utility of the rod depend upon the end that falls to one's share. As Washington Irving says, "I never could be brought to my father's mind upon that matter."

The conference meeting smiled audibly, which didn't please my professional friend, who emphatically remarked,

"I like, well enough, to hear a strong-minded woman talk, but I'd be mighty sorry to marry one."

"Set your mind at ease upon *that* matter, sir. You have no need for anxiety. Be sure that none but a weak-minded woman will ever say *yes* to *you*."

"Hit him again," mumbled a member of the conference meeting, whose sympathies had been plainly manifested at the outset, on the "other side." It is one of the sure characteristics of your true Western American that above all things he enjoys watching a fight, and seeing somebody "cracked."

"Oh," growled M. D., "*you'd* like to have *your* wife support you, would you?"

"Certin," answered the long-legged fellow assailed, firing *his* salute of tobaco juice. "Certin," he answered, meditatively, "if I was such a derned mean cuss as not to be able to take care of *my*self."

At which the conference meeting smiled again, and my professional friend retired to his silence and left me to mine.

"Never you mind," said long legs, consolingly and admiringly, and firing a fresh salute in honor of the sentiment, "*you'll* get as many husbands as *you* want, that's dead sure;" and so retired to *his* silence, leaving me to a wondering meditation on human nature till I reached Ann Arbor and content.

Every professional who has faced the Ann Arbor boys must wish them well. College students are not always desirable acquisitions to community, nor agreeable companions, nor hearers, but there is something in the presence of these youngsters as good as a cordial.

They are jolly, but they are gentlemen, full of pranks, but also full of good sense and kindliness.

The university boasts divers feminine students and the young fellows exhaust politeness on them. "Hats off," they bawl, when the girls appear, and "hats off" it is in every sense.

Also the men of the medical department are covering themselves with honor by the way they have received the women who have knocked at their doors—a marked contrast to the M. D.'s elsewhere, full fledged and hatching.

One of these from a neighboring town vouchsafed me some enlightenment which I transfer, for the benefit of whom it may concern.

"It is simply shocking," he remarked, "to thrust a woman, or to have her force herself into the gloom, the danger, and the responsibility of a sick room."

"As a nurse she now endures far more of the gloom, is exposed to greater and more protracted danger, certainly shares the responsibility, and often more than halves the help, while she gains next to none of the profit, and none at all of the honor of the doctor," objected I.

"That is a different matter," responded he, sententiously. "Beside, the nurse is not exposed to the necessity of delicate consultations with coarse and vulgar men."

"But the woman lying ill and helpless *is* subjected to the investigation of a man whom you assert may, however skilful, be both coarse and vulgar, and assuredly the nurse has to receive her instructions, often the most minute, from these same questionable lips. *Where* is the difference ?" queried I.

"There *is* a difference," conclusively. "And however well fitted a woman *may* be to practice medicine, I think the sober sense of community will always decide it to be *inexpedient* for her to do so."

"Inexpedient ?" echoed I; "but quite right and proper for her to go on in the obscurity and hard work of a nurse's career. I have noticed, curiously enough, that some men are only struck by the *inexpediency* of work for *women*, when it may lead to profit and honor, and of the *unsuitability* of such and such work for *themselves*, when there is nothing much worth having to be got by it."

"Madame," cried my incensed friend, "take care what you say. Do you mean to accuse me of selfishness and narrow-mindedness ?"

"Well," said I, "as Joe Gargery puts it, I wouldn't go so far as to say *that*, for that's a deal to say—but it looks like it."

XXIII.

Fortunately at this ticklish moment, that bit of condensed sunshine, Professor Moses Coit Tyler, came into the ante-room, and shed such a light from his bright face and eyes as to clear all shadows of controversy.

To *him* I confided the opinion that the very best thing for some thousands of women, who are in need of work, discontented with the prospect the old paths present them, and eager to enter the overcrowded avenue of medicine, would be to train themselves thoroughly to fill a great open space that is nearly empty, and *ought* to be full—the space allotted to nurses.

A plenty of people die, or survive a long or acute illness but half alive, for want of efficient nursing.

Nursing doesn't come by nature, though there is a popular superstition to the effect that "all women are born nurses." 'Tis a gift and a fine art combined.

Death No. 2 often follows Death No. 1 because the overtasked hands of affection can find doctors a plenty, cooks a plenty, friendly *offers* a plenty, but *cannot* find real, restful help in the sick room.

Nursing ought to be lifted to the dignity of a regular profession, with its schools and its students and its degrees. And the schools need *crowding*.

Preëminently in this land of bad cooking and dyspepsia.

Or, better, let us have schools for cookery over against the schools for medicine and perhaps the former would increase on the *de*crease of the latter.

Certainly whoso will establish culinary colleges in this land of market wealth and kitchen poverty, will deserve the benedictions of his kind.

If some of the women who at death bestow of their store on theological seminaries and schools that are for the exclusive benefit of men (that woman, for instance, who left $300,000 for the establishment of a chair of science in an institution already richly endowed, the doors of which are slammed in the face of any petticoated applicant)—if some such women would establish schools wherein should be taught every household and domestic art, they would deserve canonization at the hands of a long-suffering and professedly civilized though really unenlightened world.

XXIV.

Here is the suggestion of a theme for some of the "conservative" sisters who persist in the inconsistent proceeding of speech-making.

Once upon a time I did listen to such an one, and, the speaker being done, felt like passing upon her the old lady's verdict upon her new pastor's sermon—that "it was neither edifyin' nor divertin'."

I confess to a lack of patience with that sort of woman.

A woman who really believes that her place is at home—and *stays* there—is to be respected. But a woman who makes speeches to prove that a woman has no right to speak, who rushes on to platforms to denounce the appearance of women on the platform, who harangues audiences to demonstrate that the only proper sphere for woman is the fireside, and the only suitable work domestic cares, is beneath both argument and contempt.

There is neither consistency, nor reason, nor conscience in such a course.

"Well, I must say," ejaculated a well-dressed man in front of me, to a well-dressed woman at his side, "that I like what she has to say. I'm sick of the talk of these strong-minded thinkers about 'working girls,' and 'new avenues of labor,' and 'better pay.' For my part I quite agree with her that women are best off at home. I am sure that is more sensible than earning their own living."

"And so am I," responded she of the velvet and point.

"Starve!" cried the Princess Royal, while the hungry mob of Paris was howling at the palace gates. "Starve! Why I would eat *bread* first."

Exactly.

But then the bread, good friends, and how to *make* it?

"That's a fine thing Mrs. H. is doing with her husband's business," I heard one man say to another as I was tramping up and down a depot platform waiting for a delayed train. "She's making matters about as comfortable round her as she had 'em while H. was living. Queer, too, for of course she didn't know any thing about trade; but women, some of 'em at least, do have a sort of knack at emergencies."

"That's so," responded masculine No. 2. "I've often noticed it. They do things, and for the life of them they can't tell you *how*. It's what people call *intuition*, I suppose."

And *that* matter was settled.

As the world in general settles the question of how women can be by nature wholly unfit for independence and responsibility, and yet here and there, through nature alone, shoulder them strongly and successfully.

"I have an hour to spare before this belated train appears," said I to myself, "and I will improve it by hunting up this Mrs. H. and hearing *her* version of labor and triumph."

I found her, and she told me of her struggles and her achievements. Of how she had been for years her husband's "silent partner," and knew as much of the business and the books as did the active head of the firm, and of what crowded days and taxed head and hands were the basis of the "handsome living" of herself and her children, and, in parenthesis, of what happiness and content sat down in her life because of its fulness.

"Inspiration;" "Intuition;" "She did it, she didn't know how" — soothing balm for the hurt vanity of some men and women, delusion and snare to many a young girl who wishes to accomplish great results, without the fatigue or pain of protracted effort.

Investigate the lives of these successful women, scrutinize their histories, and you will find that chart and compass were thoroughly studied before they ventured against wind and tide to navigate great waters. That often through prodigies of effort they secured the same discipline and training freely accorded men; the same rooting and grounding in A B C ere they attempted to read in a hurly-burly of noise, where not alone *loudness*, but *clearness* is needed to command attention. They *learned* their work before they *did* it.

It is a pleasing theory cherished by silliness and selfishness, vanity and ignorance, folly and prejudice, that these women came up, as they have decided *all* women are to come up—like daisies.

But human beings are not daisies, do not grow like them, nor are they like them when grown. A woman does not stretch from the dirt and dark of ignorance into the full bloom and splendor of knowledge and power, simply by letting her alone, with a bit of sunshine and air, often without even these.

XXV.

And first of all she herself must know, not only that she wishes to *grow*, but after what fashion of growth.

So many girls come to me with the same query, *What* can they do? Dissatisfied, insufficiently employed at home, with no need of such employment, and with hearty dislike of it, but with no clear conception of what they can do, or even have the desire to do. With no comprehension of what it is to sit down with themselves alone, and make the acquaintance of their own *capacities* as well as their own *needs*.

An overwhelming desire to do and a distinct tendency toward doing, are nearly always "a leading," and an *opening* as well.

"I want to do *something*, I don't know what."

Nothing will come of it.

"I know what I want to do, and have a will to do it."

Something worth while comes of it.

"Fortune is the measure of intelligence," Rachel was fond of saying. Had she added earnestness and will, the definition would have been complete.

"Meanwhile," did I hear you say—"meanwhile what of homes? You want to stir in the minds of all our girls discontent with domesticity."

So?

As Mr. Lincoln would say, that reminds me of a little story.

One evening I was, naturally enough, pleased by the absorbed intensity of gaze with which through the evening I was watched by a pair of lovely brown eyes set in the fair young face of a girl directly in front of me.

I always have had, and always will have, a weakness for young girls. They are charming. I delight in them as I would in a lovely picture full of delicious tints, or a rose or amber-hued cloud in a summer sky. This one looked like a pansy, and as I watched her I hoped she was as happy and sheltered as one.

"Might I speak to you, dear Miss Dickinson, just a moment?" said a soft little voice, at the ante-room door, the evening's work being done.

"Surely, my child," answered I, stroking her pretty brown hair.

"I would like some advice, if you please, and it isn't too much trouble."

"Speak your whole mind, my infant," I replied.

"Well, then," smiling and blushing and stammering all together, "I am engaged—to be married—oh! I am not so young," in answer to a look—"almost nineteen, and I love—*him*—dearly; and we *were* to be married soon—in the spring—but—"

"But what, my dear?"

"You see—I don't know—*There!* if I stumble so you will think me a fool. I have been reading the *Woman's Journal*, and I went to hear Mrs. Livermore, when she was here last month—*such* a good lecture! and I have been wondering whether I ought not to give up the idea of marrying, and *do* something for women, and I'm not sure I could do any thing but talk, and I'm afraid I wouldn't make a very good lecturer," with a little laugh; "and yet I *should* like to help the poor women who are not so well off as I—and I've grown troubled and snarled up over it, and, as I watchd you to-night, I thought I would come and ask *you*. What would *you* advise?"

"In the whole world, my girl, what would *you* rather do?"

"Oh, I'd rather get married!—there, that does sound so selfish—but you see——"

"Yes," I assented, "I see. And you want my advice? Yes? Then, get married, by all means."

"And not try to lecture?"

"Well, no, I think not."

"But I *would* like to do something for women," she whispered, with tears in her tender brown eyes.

"So you can, my dear little heart," answered I, "by growing to the largest, noblest womanhood of which you are capable. That will help all women—and all men—who come near you, and help the cause you want to serve by showing what a woman can *be* in the world. If you want a "mission," I find there are plenty of housekeepers, but very few *home-makers*. *There* is something to do and an example to set."

"Oh, I see, I see," cried the sweet voice, "I can be happy and helpful too. *Oh!* I'm so glad!"

"So am I, and thank *you*, Miss Dickinson," said a hearty voice, and a brown hand was thrust into the doorway, followed by a fine manly young fellow, blessed by the clearest of blue eyes, lighting a frank sun-burned face. "You're a brick. Please to shake hands. I'll give my vote for *you* when you run for President, and no mistake."

At which we all laughed, the sober dominie who had "introduced me," and who had just reappeared on the field of action, included, and everybody went away satisfied, and I hope my advice was the "correct thing," and will be accounted unto me for righteousness.

XXVI.

Certainly, thought I, as I took my mail from the hands of the good dominie in whose care it had been sent, whatever other afflictions may befall her, at least she has escaped *this*.

She will not have her good nature tried by the reading of such an effusion as:

"MADAME:
"Last night I read your biography, and, though a perfect stranger, it compels me to write to you.

"I cannot give you a plausible reason for thus intruding on you, yet I cannot rest satisfied without addressing you. I do not wish to be complimentary or become a critic, but I should like to know if you are conscious of deserving the laudation which has followed you. Men and women have been great before the world that were humble in private. This, I fear, you are not.

"Those speeches of yours seem to me mercenary and unbecoming a woman. Glory, glory is beautiful, but happiness and contentment are gifts from heaven.

"I shall not apologize for writing you thus. In your position you need discipline. Take this from one who hopes it will serve that good purpose.

"I am,
"Dear madame,
"Yours most respectfully,
"———— ————."

And if her good nature bears the strain of such "discipline" as this, she will not be subjected to the pistol-to-head process after this wise:

"DEAR MISS DICKINSON:

"No doubt you will be surprised at receiving this letter from an entire stranger. I do not know you, and yet I write without any hesitation, since you profess always to be such a friend to woman I am sure you will be glad to help me.

"I set up a millinery at ———, but didn't do well and sold out and came here. I was told it was a good business town, but somehow *I* haven't prospered here. I am in debt and I need new stock, and I think if I could move into a larger store it would be better for my business, and if I could go to New York myself to buy stock and look around at the theatres, etc., for a week or two, I should like it, and it would do me good.

I need $2000, but I suppose you have a great many people asking you to help them, and I *can* get along and pay my debts and take a holiday and get a start again with $1800, and I should like to have it, on account of the spring trade, not later than next week. I am sure you will be glad to know what to do with some of your money so as to be sure it will be doing good.

"Truly yours,

"———— ————."

P.S.—I do not like checks. Please to be sure to send a draft on New York.

2d P.S.—Of course you understand I want you to *give* this, and not to *lend* it.

Though to be sure if she said "yes" to many such requests as the following, she could say "no" to the "drafts" with a clear conscience and an empty pocket:

"Mrs. Anna Dickinson :

"*Dear Miss :*—Wishing to inquiere of you I write, to tell you my Story, that we have built an A. M. E. church in Z—, and are some in debt yet, and I wish to get your concent to come to speek for us one or too evenings as a Donation, except your expenses.

"Please give us a call. Write soon.

"Yours truly,

"———— ————."

Though, to be sure, even these would not terrify her, if she were possessed of the same spirit as the sister upon whose epistle I fell last of all, fortunately, for a night's sleep was a good thing to take after *its* perusal.

Thus it ran:

"MISS

"*Dear friend* I wish A little advise of you I have got a common education but I am A good reader in 1840 I married A farmer and have four children boys I thought if I could Lecture and could make any thing I would like it better than this I get so tired of cooking and waiting on boys all the time they are so noisy that I do not enjoy myself with them I never have lectured but have been invited too ever since I was a child I would like to try but I thought it would be better to go away to commence and I thought it would be better to go with somebody, and I think it looks better for women to go together and as I never got up before A crowd it would be better to have some lectures written if you could write some for me and send them I could learn them and then I could go with you awhile and if I could do well I would like to go West for I have A great many relations there I believe we could get large crowds and I believe it would pay handsomely please answer this and let me know how much it will cost me to get started in and what you will charge me for to give me a start.

"Yours truly,

"———— ————."

That mail was mild to one that befell me at ————, where my mind, morals, person, and estate, came under the inspection and condemnation I should think of the *whole* town. If not, then at least that town can boast of divers persons of varying tastes who are nevertheless possessed of one taste in common : that of speech, explicit and corrective. For the morning after my lecture, these notes straggled into my room :

"Miss Dickinson : While listening to your lecture in this place last evening I conceived the idea of dropping you a note requesting correspondence. I am aware that I am violating the laws of custom and perhaps transcending the rules of propriety, but trust you will pardon when you know my motive.

"It would be little to say I was well pleased with the manner of your lecture, so well pleased as to greatly regret the insufficiency of the matter. You are evidently in earnest, but do not know enough of the subject about which you are speaking.

"I should like to enter upon a correspondence with you for the sake of enlightening you, broadening your views, and helping you to conclusions that a woman's mind unaided would never be able to attain.

"I will not apologize for this intrusion, feeling sure that you are sufficiently interested in the theme you present to be willing to accept instruction from better informed sources, and I am, dear madame, etc., etc.,

"———— ————."

So much for the *matter*. At least I was permitted by my modest censor to felicitate myself on the *manner* of my discourse, a short-lived felicity that died with the opening of the next epistle :

"MISS ANNA DICKINSON :

"*Dear madame :*—As you are a volunteer in the correction of abuses and faults, I feel justefied in constituting myself your adviser in regard to your way of speaking. I heard you last evening and I liked all you had to say, and indorse it fully. Go on. You are right. Only I wish you would change your way of speaking and would wear something more cheerful looking than a black silk dress. You stand so independently, and talk in such a loud voice (tho' to be sure I don't see how you could very well be heard if you spoke in a low one), that it doesn't seem to me what I would call womanly, and your appearance is too strong-minded. You are young yet and you ought to make yourself more attractive looking by wearing bright colors and ribbons and such things.

"A man who is your well-wisher,
" ——— ———."

"For all, even small favors, good Lord, make us thankful," I mumbled ; "he 'indorses' me and desires me to 'go on' even if I persist in advancing in a sad-colored, strong-minded gown. I am fortified for the next document !"

But I wasn't, for it read :

"Miss Anna—Please do not wear the long traleing dress when you Lecture. It is unbecomeing in you as a Reformer and a Professedly Sensable woman.

"Read the Tract inclosed. A word to the wise is sufficient.

"Yours,

"—— ——."

But how if I be not wise?

And wise I am not, nor acceptable to the judgment of my next mentor, whose communication, if not the epitome of wisdom, at least carries brevity—the soul of wit.

Thus it ran to its speedy climax:

"Miss Anna Dickinson:—You are a snob.

"A Working Man.

"P.S.—*Of course* (as you will say) I am a Trades Unionist."

Alas, thought I, as I eyed the last screed that lay unopened on the table, is that too a masculine outpouring? More reforming and correcting and criticizing? If it be, I shall go down, swamped helplessly and hopelessly under the deluge. Why did I try to help these beings so more than able to take care of themselves, while they assist and enlighten me?

Is it from a man?

Let us see ——
Yes.

Who knows? perhaps it will be so pleasant, or friendly, or frank, or kindly, as to quite put the others out of sight, and make forgetfulness of them ensue?

It did.

Said my friend:

"God has blessed you with a vigorous and thinking mind and ability to talk it out, and now are you not under very strong obligations to devote your talents to his service?

"What shall it profit you, my dear madame, if you gain the whole world and lose your own soul? Soon all you will need of earth will be a shroud and a coffin.

"You must be amassing property rapidly, but it is not safe from moth and rust. Permit me to ask, Have you treasure hid where rust doth not corrupt? As I looked at you last night I feared not. You seemed too much interested in pressing home truths that are only to benefit the material prosperity of men.

"'Seek ye first the kingdom of heaven.'

"I am the pastor of a small church now in its infancy in the neighboring town of ——. In the work of building, my people have become involved in debt—a debt that is now due and must be paid. In addition to which they are in arrears for my salary to the amount of two hundred dollars.

"'The laborer is worthy of his hire.'

"You receive a liberal patronage from an admiring and delighted public. Don't forget the poor.

"Out of the season you can certainly afford us one evening. Other places must furnish you *cash*. We will give you what is better—our prayers.

"If you are not willing to come you can do as good service perhaps by sending on as a donation to the cause of Christ the amount—two hundred dollars—now due me by my people.

"'He who giveth to the poor lendeth to the Lord.'

"I have understood that you are a Quaker, or Friend as they call themselves, which body, I believe, are a sort of infidels, but of whatever faith or unfaith, 'the Lord loveth a cheerful giver.'

"Give us a call soon.

"Your well-wisher,

"———— ————."

I could bear no more. No? I *must*. For there on the floor where it had slipped from the companionship of bigger and clumsier envelopes lay a small messenger with face marked by feminine lines.

Comfort at last!

Was it so?

"ANNA DICKINSON: I hope you will pardon the liberty I take in addressing you. And yet it is no real liberty, and I am but doing right, and so I ask no pardon. Although my sphere is an humble one as compared with yours, yet before last evening I had thought we both had the same end in view, and were endeavoring to accomplish good, you in your corner and I in mine.

"The way to help the world is to help women. The way to elevate men is to elevate the female portion of community, and how you can waste your time on 'strikes,' and 'trades unions,' and 'apprentices,' and matters that only affect the welfare of boys and men, and yet pretend to be the champion of your sex is a mystery to such a woman as me.

"I went last night to hear something that would be of benefit to me, and felt as though I had been cheated out of my seventy-five cents when you said nothing from the beginning to the end of the evening about the cause of woman. You didn't do your own sex any good by any thing you said, and none of the men will thank you, and if they do, *that* will be no profit to me. I want to see you and talk to you about this, and if you are going to stay in our town over the day I will call this afternoon at the hotel to see you.

"Perhaps you noticed me last evening, for I moved about some while you were speaking. I am a middle-aged woman, sat well forward in the middle aisle, the fifth bench I think, and was dressed in black with a brown hat.

"Your friend."

XXVII.

I didn't stay till afternoon. I locked my trunk, put my hat sadly on my diminished head, and left the town. Even the request of the lecture committee that I would return to the place the next season failed to put me into a cheerful and self-satisfied frame of mind. I was flattened for the day.

But laughed in spite of my depressed feelings over a queer-looking bridal pair who boarded the train at ——. The groom, gorgeous in lavender trowsers, gray coat, flowered waistcoat, scarlet necktie and stove-pipe hat. The bride arrayed in a pea-green suit, and blue and white bonnet.

"So you're caught at last, are you, Jack," shouted a sympathizing friend, coming up the car to shake hands with the happy man. "I congratulate you."

"Thankee, yes," assented Jack.

> "Cubit's shot me
> *And* Hyleman's got me

Fast enough! Ha! ha! Huzzah! There, you didn't know you had a poet for a husband, Maria, did you?"

And Maria blushed, and bridled, and looked about her as though she were aware she had made a great catch, and was sure she was the envy of all feminine beholders, and her Jack abundantly able to "take the shine" off of any other he, be he who he might, but would generously refrain from speech to that effect, or any noisy outward demonstrations.

And the next day I came to a little experience that more than offset all the "mashing" I had endured the day before, and set me up again.

I was trotting along to the train, when a fine, wholesome-looking matron stopped me with—

"You don't know me, but I know you and love you. God bless you. Shake hands."

Gladly I thrust out my member for the desired ceremony.

"You are very busy, I hope?".

"Yes," said I.

"Good," she responded. "Keep at it."

"Tired?"

"Sometimes," said I.

"That's right," said she. "Stick to it. It's good to get tired doing such work as you're doing. The Lord'll rest you by and by—bless you. Happy?"

"Yes," said I.

"Bless you for that," said she; and then after a bit of confab, and good-by, she called after me, "I hope you are well and hearty.'

"Yes," bawled I.

"Bless you for *that*," cried she, and so we went on our respective ways. What befell her I know not. I hope nothing but good. For me, I plunged into a hornet's nest.

XXVIII.

One of the "professional agitators" spied me in the cars, and planting himself in the forward seat, said abruptly—

"I don't like you nor your theories."

"Ah!" I responded; "fortunately I have the strength, or the brassiness of mind, to bear the weight of your displeasure."

"No," he continued. "I used to like to hear you till you took to talking of a matter you have no knowledge of, and have no business and no right to touch, and now I'd rather hiss you than listen to you *any* night. You've got no right to be talking about this workingmen's question."

"No?" I asked. "Why not?"

"To begin with, you know you're a rich woman," said he.

"Don't I wish I knew it?" interpolated I.

"And you don't know any thing about work, *practically*," he went on.

"Well," said I, "as I have taken care of myself since I was fifteen years old, I ought to know something about it—*very* practically too."

"And your sympathies are altogether with the employers. *That's* plain to be seen," he pursued.

"Have you seen it? When and where did you hear me?" inquired I.

"No, I haven't, and I wouldn't go to hear you either," answered my candid friend; "when *I* go to hear any one I like to hear somebody who knows what he's talking about, and isn't all on one side of a question, and that the wrong one."

"You are *quite* sure your favorite orator would not be a looking-glass?" I asked, "or an echo?"

"You mean I like to hear my own views, I suppose. Yes, I do, of course, because I know they're *right*, and I like to advocate them too. Now I'm a trades-unionist, and I can't see how you can dare to go about the country fighting the trades unions, and saying your say so freely on a matter that's taxed the political economists for centuries, when it's safe to say you don't know and can't know any thing about it.

"No?" queried I, "I am learning something now. So the political economists have been taxing their brains for centuries over the outrages of the trades unions, and the "Molly Maguires," have they? I thought that special class of troubles had been confined to the last fifty years, but I stand corrected. And I don't fight the trades unions, but their tyranny and abuses. I approve of *them*. And I talk about the matter because I am interested in it, and have as good an opportunity to know about it as you. *What are you?*"

"I've just told you I was a working man."

"What kind? Professional? minister? lawyer? professor? doctor? teacher?"

"No," he replied, with disdain, "I don't belong to the drones of society."

"No? Perhaps then," I farther interrogated, "you are a baker? or a butcher? or a chandler? No? Nor a farmer? nor a market gardener? nor a cattle-raiser? nor a dairyman?—none of these? Maybe a mason? a carpenter? a machinist? You can't be a factory operative? nor a day laborer?

Pardon me if I ask what *is* your trade, and where did you serve your apprenticeship ?"

The man had no trade. I knew it, but I wanted him to confess it, and he did.

He served as a good background to throw into relief some *real* workingmen I saw that evening: a body of fine-looking fellows, who had been listening with peculiar intentness to the speech. They got round me, twenty of them perhaps, and their spokesman inquired, " You disapprove of strikes always ?"

" In this country, yes," I answered, " for there is sufficient intelligence and goodwill on both sides to come to a right understanding without resorting to the stupid and brutal methods of war."

" That *sounds* fair," he said, " but I notice your solution of difficulties for such men as me and my mates is co-operation, but co-operation needs money. Now here are these men," I looked at and approved of them, not a dull nor sulky face among them. " We are machinists." I approved of them yet more. I always did have a special admiration for the combined sense and manliness that are almost invariable ingredients of this class of workers. " We want to get on in the world, we would like to be our own employers, but we haven't money."

"You look as though you had the equivalent of money—brains," said I.

They smiled and made no objection to *that*.

"You know, in this town, of men who have money to invest?"

"Yes," they assented.

"And who could know of you—what you are as men and workmen?"

"I think so. Yes," said the spokesman.

"Well, of course I don't *know*," I went on, "but I do think if you would make a plan of what you can do—how work, what per cent allow your captain—and carry it to some such man, who because he has brains and money will be able to understand and help the scheme, you could get what you want."

"What do you mean by our captain?" asked one of them.

"Your business head," I answered. "There isn't a money-making scheme in this country—factory, railroad, telegraph, bank—that is not a joint-stock affair—a co-operative effort whereby a few rich men band together and hire another man even keener and abler than they, to conduct their affairs to profit: and what five rich men can do, five hundred poor men can do, I believe equally well."

"I like to hear you say it," spoke one of the hearty voices. "It puts faith into a man. You say it as if you were sure of it."

"It's worth trying," assented another, "and we'll *try*," chorused the score.

If they did try I know their enterprise flourished, for they are the stuff out of which successes are made.

XXIX.

It is the creatures too indolent to work, vain, shallow, eager for a little brief authority, and hungry for notoriety, who are making eight-tenths of the trouble among the real working men; and the workingmen, in regard to trade government, are like the great body of the people in regard to the general government, "too busy" to look after the character and doings of those who are all too ready to be the "keepers and defenders of their interests."

"Workingmen!" Half of the fomenters of discords, leaders in strikes, union officers, spouters enthusiastic for war and its accompanying privations and miseries, are like the witness, who, being asked some questions by the Sheffield Parliamentary Commission touching his trade and its compensation, averred that he had been "on the box" for four years continuously, drawing, regularly, seventeen shillings and sixpence a week, and doing nothing but what the box-keepers told him: stirring up strikes.

"And it warn't bad wage neither," he added, cheerfully.

For their labors—they are no more productive than those of another witness, who, being asked by this same commission as to what were the precise duties of a committee man, "didn't exactly know," though he had been serving in that capacity for sixteen weeks.

"What did you do, yourself?" was inquired.

"I sat still and sooped ale."

"And what did the others do?"

"Many of them sooped ale too."

"Had then," demanded one of the investigators, "committee men no duties besides that of supping ale?"

Deponent could not say: during his sixteen weeks of office he had discovered no other.

When practical workingmen have done with

quacks and leeches, and exercise as much thought and sense on their own affairs as they now demand justice and generosity of their employers, there will be less need of the demand, and speedier and better methods of ensuring it when needed, than are seen in these days of wasteful warfare and angry recrimination.

XXX.

I had a great curiosity before reaching Boston to know what manner of treatment its audience would accord this particular theme.

A Boston "*reformatory*" audience is the kindest of all audiences—to any one it can patronize; and the most attentive—to any one who is very great, and who moves with the tide.

There is a popular superstition that it is liberal—given to candid and courageous hearing of all sides of a question—willing to listen, if not to commend.

If any person should state that the people composing it are the most intolerant liberals, and the most conservative reformers to be found by long search, the *legitimate* descendants of the Puritans who were ready to die for their *own* freedom of conscience, and more than ready to put any one to death who ventured to demand freedom of conscience as an inalienable right of all mankind, such person would run the risk of a critical stoning, or an intellectual whipping at the cart's tail, but would have the moral support to be found in his own internal consciousness of having spoken the truth.

I smiled—the sort of smile that tends to *depress* the corners of the mouth—as I watched the reception, not *hearing*, accorded the speech by the magnificent gathering in the great ungainly hall.

Among those three thousand men and women, certainly there was scarce one with brains insufficient to detect sophistry or sift testimony, or reject false argument, so that, having paid their money to hear, they could well afford to sit still and listen.

To drown speech is proof of conscious weakness to defend a right cause, and consequent unwillingness to face the strength of its opponents ; or it is a confession that the cause itself is a poor and wrong one.

Always hear the opposition, say I. If one is wrong, one has so a chance of being righted. If one is right, one has opportunity to be strengthened. And in either case one has a better show to hit his enemy if one goes out and views his position and knows where to find him.

And in any case, long live free speech! and let everybody have a fair field, favor or no favor, in which to utter it.

Not so thought ye Boston lecture audience of that night, its faith at the time being one to be formulated somewhat after this wise:—

At present, the greatest crime a man can commit is to wear clean linen and claim a liberal bank account of his own accumulation. Such an one being guilty of brains, of industry, of skill, of hard work, of exhaustless energy, and of having used these to lift himself from poverty to affluence, is in the minority, and as such has no rights that any lover of his kind, and the majority, is bound to respect.

Another crime of almost equal magnitude is for a man to prefer working the number of hours a day himself may choose, and not those that shall be marked for him by a body of fellow-workmen ; and to get all the pay for his labor to which his skill shall entitle him, instead of taking the price that the least skilled or idlest amongst his fellows is capable of commanding.

Yet another is that a man satisfied with his

work and his pay, with a family to support, and no quarrel to make with his employer, shall prefer uninterrupted industry and profit to pauper idleness that shall be commanded by a body of other laborers who are dissatisfied with their work and their pay, or with the presence of an obnoxious man or boy in their midst.

Another and worse crime is to be a poor boy in search of a trade. Woe to him! Better for him had he never been born than that he should depend for the opportunity to gain skill on the consent of men who know to the full the value of what they withhold.

And a crime as great as any of these is to protest against tyranny of all kinds, whether it be of class over class, of masters over men, or of men over masters, or of men over men, or last and worst and meanest of all, of skilled men over unskilled and helpless boys.

At present, "labor reform" is the faith and the fashion of a great many people, among whom should be numbered my audience. It is easier to talk about "bloated aristocrats" than to make manifest the truth that, in ninety-nine cases out of a hundred the capitalists of this land are the industrious, capable, hard-working laborers.

Easier to pay a man coarse compliments by calling him part of the "real bone and sinew of the nation," "one of the props of the Republic," and so secure his vote, than to show him that this sort of thing is said for the express purpose of securing his vote for some monstrous scheme of pillage, or the enriching of the sole class who, in this land, are affluent without toil. Easier to flatter a man than to tell him the truth. Easier to sympathize with the "victim of capital" than to show him how he can be his own master by skill and cooperative effort; and far easier to snivel over the oppression of the employer than to denounce the cruelty of the employed over one another, or over those who would fain be of their number, but who are by them relegated to the streets and so apprenticed to ignorance, vice, crime, the prison, and even there are denied by their workingmen tyrants a knowledge of the skilled labor that might serve as a teacher of reformation, and would certainly remove the burthen of their support from the struggling and tax-paying men and women outside.

Well, Boston turns round with the rest of the world, her "reform" audiences included. By and by they will "right face" on this matter.

But on the evening of which I tell you, as I said my say to this question, I had abundant opportunity to realize that I was in the city that had stood men in pillories, and hung women on the Common, for speaking and spending themselves, not in self-seeking, but in conscientious if disagreeable efforts for the good of their kind.

If they had hissed when I closed I would have had no objection, but to hiss before I had begun, and to hiss so persistently as to "joomble the understonding and confoond the sense," is, I respectfully submit, neither a fair nor brave way of meeting an antagonist or an argument.

XXXI.

Certainly, as a rule, it is well to let people work out their own salvation. Like the mediators in a domestic brawl, the well-intentioned folks who try to help along the good effort are apt to get no thanks, and to carry away two boxed ears, and a face swollen on both sides by way of compensation. For example: At a town—not in the moon—I found a crowd packed so long and so closely into a thrice-heated and air-tight hall as to more nearly resemble freshly scalded lobsters than human beings, and I, having compassion on them, entered a petition in their behalf for some oxygen, repeating the petition at intervals during the evening, for I liked them so well as to desire confab with them through the whole hour and a quarter, and not have them either stifle or stew during the operation.

Lo! the next morning's paper gave liberal space to divers and sundry " communications," to the effect that " Miss D. ought to have been sufficiently complimented by the presence of an immense and uncomfortable crowd of people, many of whom had been in waiting two hours before the time of the lecture, to have shown better taste and temper than she displayed by wasting their time in complaints of the air and insulting comments on the ventilation of the beautiful new hall she had the distinguished honor of opening."

Live and learn, is an *old* motto.

My rasped sensibilities were soothed by a hearty laugh, as, paper in hand, I was rushing to the cars.

A stout party, very red as to the face, very pudgy, and coarse-looking as to jewelled hands, peacock hued as to raiment, thrust her head out of an elegant coupé, and, hailing me, demanded—

" How many miles to Bosting ?"

"Seven," said I.

"Seving?" she cried, thrusting out each one of her stubby digits, panoplied in gold and diamonds, and waving a manacled arm. "*Seving* miles to Bosting? Gracious heavings! I thought it was eleving."

It was so long since the close of the war and the reign of shoddy, that I stared as though I had beheld a resurrection. I did not come sufficiently near to determine the doubt, but am next to sure that I *might* have sniffed an odor of petroleum.

XXXII.

There is one comfort in connection with a thought of such people. Solomon put it succinctly, "A fool and his money are soon parted." They serve as a good circulating medium. They keep money afloat.

And then there is the consolation to people who have not much money, as they contemplate these beings, that, there is something better than money.

One realizes that fact in migrating through a legion of small towns scattered over New England.

Nobody is rich, but nobody is poor; there is no grandee's palace, and there is no hovel; nobody rests in silken ease, but nobody is bound to the grindstone ; men are busy, women are busy, part of the time children are busy, but healthfully, not as they are in the great wearing factory towns.

There are a plenty of little houses with a gable roof or a dormer window, or a piazza, or a rustic stoop—something to suggest artistic sense as well as utility.

Inside there are painted walls, with pictures on them, prints, or lithographs, or "chromos," and painted floors, with the indescribably homely-look that comes from hand-made bright rag-rugs and patchwork cushions on the old-fashioned rocking-chairs and settees. There is that abomination, an air-tight wood stove, but then, to offset it, there is always a red moreen curtain, or some bright bindings among the books, or a scarlet or golden flower burning against the ivy growing about the window.

There are churches, and schoolhouses, and the town hall, and generally a lyceum hall, and a lyceum, and library or reading-room, and there are people to look after all these, who are honest and earnest to the core, and faithful " to their lights," and diligent searchers after truth.

Some enthusiastic but untrained youth, who has been reading about Sam Adams, writes me from western wilds, "Is there any other beings that does any more toward keeping this wicked world as good as it is, and is there any other class of people that is any honester than the Yankees?"

On the whole, I am free to confess that I think there "isn't."

Not abounding in ludicrous experiences to enliven the road of a tired traveller, yet even in the midst of *its* staidness, now and again I stumbled upon some "richness."

XXXIII.

Appropriately enough, at Salem I found my ghost.

Salem is an antique and pleasingly suggestive town, full of present beauty and past memories.

Perhaps it was by reason of a glance given that afternoon at "Witches' Hill," and a remembrance of the ugly tree that once cast dismal shadows there, that I did not laugh quite honestly, when, in the evening, my hostess remarked, "I presume you know that this house has the reputation of being haunted."

"Is it so?" I inquired. "By witch or Quaker? Angry or friendly ghost? And does the spirit show itself to earthly vision, or is it content to 'demonstrate' by noise alone?"

"By noise alone," said my hostess, "and enough of it. There are all manner of mysterious sounds to be heard in this house o' nights. Sometimes by daylight too."

"Rats," said my host, sententiously, adding, "They come from the old warehouse next door."

My hostess smiled.

"Men always *do* think they know so much," she remarked, blandly, "*I've* heard noises that no rat made."

"Wind," suggested the offending skeptic.

"Very like," assented his wife, "if *spirits* are made of wind.

I thought I detected some light-minded words in connection with "spirits," but remembering mine host was a staunch advocate of prohibition concluded my ears had deceived me.

"You are not superstitious, I hope," said he.

"I hope you are not timid," said she.

"Neither the one nor the other," stoutly asseverated I.

"Good," said he.

"You will be apt to hear something," said she.

"Very well," said I. "What is written is written. If sights and sounds of ghosts be stamped in the book of my fate, I must submit to what is in store for me," and I went away to my room.

The room was a delightful old-fashioned apartment, big enough for three modern sleeping concerns, the open fire, and huge chintz-covered easy chair inviting—I said I wouldn't—yet even while I said so, sat down to read.

I read and the hours wore on.

The book was not cheerful, far from it, but it was fascinating—Bulwer's "Strange Story"—and as the night waned there was something more than the sinking fire to account for the chill that insidiously crept over me.

I could hear the striking of the bell at the town hall. Two o'clock. It *did* sound preternaturally clear and loud. I paused in my reading to listen. *Could* the unhappy souls that so many years ago were untimely sped into Eternity yet wander about these old haunts of earth to disturb the descendants of their merciless executioners? I pondered the thought, and, still pondering, put down the book with its weird characters and uncanny apparitions, and found my way, shiveringly and in haste, to bed.

Had I really been asleep? I do not know. I know a longer or shorter interregnum of dark and silence had followed the extinguishing of my light, and that I had lost consciousness when *something* wakened me.

Up I sprang with the familiar exclamation, "Who's there?"

No reply, but a *swishing* sound, soft and continuous, smote my ear in such wise as to make it tingle with any thing but pleasing sensations.

"Who's there?" again demanded I, this time defiantly.

Again no answer, but stillness fell for a space.

Softly I got out of bed, and, as well as I could, steered for the gas-burner and the match safe with intent to cast some light upon the matter, but alas, was foiled on reaching them by the discovery of one headless stick and two burned ones.

The silence continued.

"Sheer imagination," said I to myself jeeringly, and retraced my steps through the room.

Swish, swish, went the noise, and I sat up again—*swish, swish, swish.*

Rats? No; it was not like rats. No gnawing, no scamper, no patter.

Wind? Perhaps so. There is no accounting for some of *its* demonstrations. I shook up the pillow and composed myself to sleep once more.

It was no use—*swash* went something.

I scrambled out this time in dire earnest. A light I must have. A light I *would* have. There were no matches. I stumbled my way to the hall door, and cautiously opened it. No light. No stir. No possibility of illumination from that quarter, and as for rousing any one by my prowlings in search of match or candle my dignity would not allow of such a suggestion—no, not for a moment. Had I not emphatically repelled the insinuation of either timidity or superstition? I shut the door and turned back into the room.

Seemingly the fire had died, but I found my way to the grate and poked at it gingerly, till through the ashes I saw the glimmering hint of an ember, and blew at it till my throat was dry, in a vain effort to light a scrap of paper, dragged from the recesses of my coat pocket, but the letter-paper was harsh and unamenable to fire or reason, and did but smoke and smoke till, through heating and charring, it was gone without consenting to the dawn of a blaze.

The noise had stopped meanwhile, but began again. A soft breathing and a movement like trailing garments. I had no more paper to help me. I must prosecute my investigations in the dark.

For the second time I stumbled to the door. No one there. To the windows. There were four of these, lofty, with blinds within and without. No, no tree branch grew sufficiently near to strike against them. No loose hinge nor ill-hung sash permitted them to waver, no rain fell from the darkened sky to beat against them, but the darkened sky and dreary night allowed no friendly glimmer to penetrate the gloomy recesses of my room, up and down which I navigated, hands and feet both in requisition, with many a halt and more than one threatened shipwreck in a hopeless voyage of discovery.

Nothing but darkness, stillness, and bruises rewarded me. "I am a fool," then said I, with chattering teeth; "my death I shall catch, but a ghost?—no. Let us have done!"

Swash went the something once more.

"Ah ha!" whispered I, with malicious triumph, as I shuffled across the room; "you are there, are you? in the water pitcher? trying to drown yourself? *Now* I have you!" and I plunged my hand into the pitcher, into the basin, back into the pitcher to its bottom. Nothing there but water, cold and plenteous — nothing found save a wet arm and an addition to discomfort by a wet sleeve.

I went back to the grate, and sat down on the floor in front of it, thinking its memories might warm me, and resolved myself into a committee of one for farther thought and the consideration of fresh tactics for a new campaign.

"There is nothing amiss here," finally announced the committee, embracing itself and blowing vigorously on its frozen fingers.

A sound, not noisy, but unmistakable, replied.

The committee applied its ear to the floor till it was satisfied and its back ached. The visitant did not occupy there. The committee decided on a pilgrimage, and glued its ear to each of the four walls successively till it tingled with the cold and strain. The unknown guest was not quartered there.

Guest indeed! Who was to say it was not the lawful inhabitant of this domain justly incensed by an impudent interloper's calling of committees and sitting in judgment upon its peaceful if nocturnal ablutions and exercise? The committee, rebuked, hung its head in shame, and resolved itself into the humility of a private citizen.

The private citizen, unsupported by official authority, retreated to the shelter of pillows and blankets, and determined to give repose to its heavy head and burning eyeballs, though a whole legion of ghosts saw fit to revel in what had once been the abode of some one of their number, or the habitation of a contemporary persecutor or friend.

Determination has its rewards. Strained eyeballs and tense head gradually relaxed, frozen body thawed, sleep, with its downy mantle, was covering all fret and fatigue with its blessed oblivion, when— Well, I sat up once more, descended, ran nimbly, for I had learned every step of the way to the grate, and that forlorn hope of an ember. Did it still live? Barely, and fast growing cold.

There were no more scraps of paper, no more letters. Even the match-sticks had been tried in desperation and tried in vain; but there was my pocket-book, and some scrip, or, this failing, a bill of inferior denomination. So the blowing, and the ashes, and the slow dull smoking, slower, and duller than before, were repeated, and that was all—save that I was the poorer by some scrip and a greenback or so.

"Miserable ghost!" cried I, the necessity of speech subdued by reason of the living beings sleeping in near rooms, making speech doubly intense not to say savage—to the being, living or dead, but wide-awake and aggressive in my own room — "miserable ghost, speak or be silent, prance or be still. I will sacrifice to you no more time, no more rest, no more comfort, no more letters, no more greenbacks. I defy you—only, for my own enlightenment will you, in return for the annoyance you have caused me, in ghostly language tell me whether you go through this performance every night, and whether you purpose continuing it till morning? Three raps for affirmative. One for denial. Come! Begin!"

It began, but not as I desired. It was not a ghost to be defied, nor a spirit to indulge in trifling conversation, and it punished my effrontery by going on with its dreary programme as though it entirely ignored me and my queries. No light-minded rapping responded, but, in its stead, a curious gurgling sound that to my intent ear seemed like the breath of a person dying by slow suffocation.

Yes, it is true; my hair certainly *did* uncurl, and each particular thread did stand on end with horror. Small, cold claws paced down my back, and marked off each spinal vertebra with painful and peculiar distinctness. My chest was a drum, and my heart a drum-stick that beat a double tattoo with as much ease as though it had been two.

I ceased alike entreaties and defiance. There were no more observations to be made. I would not speak to the inhabitants of my own world, though the vertebra parted, and each hair turned white where it stood. I got into my bed with a desperate determination to *remain* there, and I remained till morning.

Morning came. There was nothing at the windows, nothing at the door, on the furniture, behind the furniture, under the bed—nothing in the pitcher, the basin—nothing *anywhere!*

I struck against the porcelain foot-bath, unstumbled against and unremembered the night before, and screamed—in a voice that brought the household to my threshold—over a half-grown, half-drowned rat, that was swish, swishing with its wretched little claws up the concave side of the slippery ware and sliding back into its unwished-for bath of ten inches of cold and mustardy-water.

I screamed, but it was morning. My reputation for *courage* was lost, but no one of that household has known of cause to accuse me of *superstition* unto this day.

XXXIV.

Surviving the infliction and affliction of my ghostly visitant, not many nights later I thought mine hour had come, by reason of the tenacity of one human, or *de*-human man.

The place in which he found me is one of the delightfully quaint towns that are strewn all along the coast line of New England, full of old-fashioned streets and houses and furniture and people. Nobody is in haste. Nobody is guilty of the indecorum of noise. The carving and gilding of picture and mirror frames, the spindle legs of tables and chairs are ceaseless proofs of the antique propriety and quietude of the people; a good strong whiff of the material air that blows in towns near at hand, the emphatic movements of the modern man and woman, would send carving and gilding, backs and legs, tables and chairs, into an indistinguishable heap together.

To the shelter of one of these enchanting old houses went I. Mahogany door, half a foot thick, rivalling in shine its grinning dragonhead of a brass knocker. Wide hall hung with prints yellowed by years in ebony and walnut frames odd and old, and bits of furniture of such long-past fashion as to appear new, but with a flavor of age about them that no imitation, however admirable, could emulate. Opening on either side from the ample expanse of the hallway, a half dozen rooms, each more charming than the other, with its china and pictures and nondescript articles that are as much for ornament as use, and for use as ornament. The curtains and carpets of rooms and hall and stairway delicious in the soft richness of their faded hues.

My hostesses, three snowy-haired delicate-featured, soft-speaking, noiseless-motioned, slight, silk-clad, dainty, old ladies, served by two ancient and faithful maidens and one faithful and ancient coachman, and "chore" man who abode in some other region.

Into this sedate and pleasing domicile had

entered and taken possession an element strange and foreign, a big-bodied, red-headed, strident-voiced, rampant son of Anak, the President of the Lecture Association at ——, where I was due in a few evenings.

This society and the society with which my engagement stood for the following evening, without consulting me, had quietly exchanged dates, and were so good as to inform me at the last moment of their little arrangement.

To keep the appointments in their original order would be to rest through an undisturbed night, leave at a reasonable season the next day, and travel for a half dozen of hours.

To meet the new requirements necessitated a call at three o'clock in the morning, a ride of forty miles on a cattle train, exposed to filth and bitter storm, a run across Boston, breakfastless, to another train, a broken ten hours'—part journey, part wait—thereafter.

Had I been guilty of the folly of making such an engagement, I should have kept it though its fulfilment had involved a ride of *all* night instead of but the portion of one, an association with cattle as well as the occupancy of a cattle box, and a dinnerless afternoon added to a breakfastless morning; but as I had nothing to do with the planning of the reasonable programme, I naturally declined having any thing to do with its execution.

In noisy and affable wise my strident-voiced friend set forth his plans and purposes, and having done so, rose to leave with the thoughtful announcement, "Give yourself no uneasiness about getting off in time. *I'll* be sure to call you. Loud enough too! Ha! ha! never fear! Rout out the old ladies at the same time. Do 'em good to give 'em such an early start. Got any orders?"

"None," I said, "save that you are not to come at all."

"Oh, but I will. Trust me for *that*. You mightn't be dead sure to get awake, you know."

"I don't intend to go, nor to get awake either," said I.

"Of course you don't," went on the trumpet, "of course you don't. Women never *do* know their own minds, but you'll be all ready when the times, *I* know. Now just listen," and he proceeded to re-narrate the whole cheerful and comfortable plan. "Do you understand?" blared he at its close.

"Yes," I answered. "I am not an idiot. I understand so well that there can be no doubt as to my absolute refusal to have any thing to do with it."

"My dear," said a sweet old treble, "won't you come and take your cup of coffee now? It is getting late. This gentleman," the shadow of a shade of stress on the word, "will doubtless excuse you."

"Certin, ma'am, certin," blew the trumpet. "I'm a plain man. Don't stand on any ceremony with *me*. Miss Anna can drink her coffee —though coffee isn't wholesome—whenever she wants to, and I'll just step out with her and settle this little matter while she's drinking it."

Out went he and recited again his attractive lesson.

"There is no use, sir," objected I, "in wasting time and effort to induce me to carry out a foolish plan in which I have had and will have no part. You have broken our contract, insulted me, wronged your audience, and now reasonably expect me to destroy my comfort and jeopardize my throat and voice, and through them a dozen following engagements, to make good your folly. I will have nothing to do with the matter."

"Now look here, Miss Anna," broke in the thunderous voice, " there ain't no use in your losing your temper. 'Tain't becoming *in* a young woman, nor *to* a young woman, and you might just as well hold your horses. *I'll* come round here by half-past two o'clock, and rout you out, and you'll have time to think better of it by that. Here, Maria—that's what the old lady called you, ain't it?—just hand *me* a cup of coffee."

The ancient and faithful serving maiden *looked* at him! If looks could kill! Unfortunately—at times unfortunately—they *can't.*

"Maria," said the sweet old treble, with a little tremble and the slightest suggestion of staccato appearing in it together—" Maria, if Miss Dickinson is through with the coffee, carry it to the kitchen, and then show her to her room."

"Well! that's cool! ha! ha!" roared the irrepressible. "Ain't inclined to hospitality? All right. I've had my supper. I only thought it would be more sociable to take a cup with Miss Anna here. Now come, Miss Anna, just you listen to reason;" and he fell to demonstrating it or its reverse once more.

"My dear," said another of the gentle old

ladies, "I will go to your room with Maria, and leave this person to his own devices."

"All right, ma'am," consented our sensitive friend. "He's able to take care of himself. Don't mind *me*," and the last seen of him, as we retreated, was of a face and figure apparently intent on a notebook and some memoranda.

He got out of the house. *How* he got out of the house I cannot testify, but that he went was manifest both from his absence when I returned to the scene of our fray, and from his presence, big, burly, and red, on the front seat of the town hall when I reached it.

He was not a helpful element in the audience. He cheered too much, and chuckled too much, and was too exasperatingly and conspicuously patronizing. There are limitations to all tempers, *even* a lyceum lecturer's.

I being done, like a Jack in the box up sprang fiery head and began it all over, as though what he had to say contained a large ingredient not alone of good sense but of absolute novelty.

"I will not go," had been my first speech. My last was, "I will say nothing more to you."

"Just as well," consented my tormentor. "There ain't any more *needs* saying as I see.

I'll be round for you at half-past two, *sharp*, so you can sleep sound as you please until then. Good-night, Miss Anna. Good-night, ma'am; it's a pity *you'll* have to be wakened too, but I guess it won't hurt you," and the full-grown imp put a fresh straw into his mouth, stuck his hands into his outside pockets, and marched away.

"He will not dare," cried the three gentle voices, as we sat about the friendly, round supper-table with its lavender-scented damask, and exquisite china, and bountiful old-fashioned delicacies.

"I should like to see him!" remarked Maria, in a tone that indicated it would be ill with the object contemplated if her eyes were forced to such inspection.

The dear delight that followed! The dear delight of sitting in a room filled with an atmosphere of sweet content and quiet goodness and refinement, permeating and pure as the smell of treasured rose-leaves; of looking into the glowing heart of that friendly companion—an open fire; of hearing tales of the old, old time from lips that added a grace almost pathetic to the cheerful and weird stories told; of telling in turn to ears that gave hospitable welcome, incident and experience of a life as foreign to this life as a crowded and dusty race-course would be to the inhabitants of a peaceful convent, while a November gale blew without, and the far-off sound of the sea boomed in at intervals, solemn and grand.

Midnight's mystic hour went by unheeded, and one o'clock sounded from the old clock on the stairs before the clear trebles chorused a "good-night, my child," and Maria, for the second time, carefully marshalled me to my room, and having poked the fire, and peered into the pitchers, and given a shake to the curtains, and ineffectually striven to gaze out into the storm, remarked, "I hope you'll sleep well," and added, with her hand on the door knob and with an ominous shake of a brass candlestick, "I'd like to see him!"

I laughed, forgot the annoyance of the early evening, dreamed over the delight that followed, listened to the winds and the waves and the tremendous voices of the night, till I fell into slumber, peaceful and profound.

Was the house on fire? Had the sea broken its bounds? Were all the floods out? Thud! thud! thud! The windows rattled! The room trembled! Had the end of time come?

No, only the old man of the sea had risen and clambered to Sinbad's back once more.

He battered, and banged, and thumped, and roared, flung stones at the glass, shook the knobs, thundered with the knocker, beat his weight against the door, shouted, apostrophized, yelled, danced a war-dance in the street, and raised a war-whoop through the air.

Neighbors there were none near, police were afar, or the disturber of night's repose *might* have met a fate he richly merited. As the case stood, he demonstrated till he was weary, paused for breath and energy, and speedily, all too speedily recuperated, returned afresh to his desperate deeds.

"It is infamous," cried I at last. "I will no longer by silence consent to this outrage upon these poor little women and their peaceful abode," and flew off my couch to devise methods of vengeance, when a fine, small voice said,

"Are you awake, my dear?"

Was I awake!

"Rather," answered I, sententiously and inelegantly. "Very much awake."

"I hope you are not frightened, my child," chimed in another sweet old flute.

"Don't pay any attention to him," cried a companion third. "Don't light your lamp. Don't make any sign. Don't give the horrible creature the satisfaction of knowing he has disturbed any of us."

It was too much. I burst out laughing. "He knows we are not *stone* deaf," I objected.

"Hush—sh—sh," breathed a chorus. "He might hear you—" There was noise enough of tempest with his own uproar to have drowned the voice of a cannon. "*Don't* let him hear you. It might please him. Be as patient as you can, dear child. We will go back again," and the beneficent white-robed visitants vanished.

The "band began to play" and the "animals to perform" anew with added fervor and fury, and continued unweariedly. 2.45 was called; 3, 3.10, 3.15, 3.20, 3.25, 3.30. A cessation.

Let us hope he is dead, or has fainted, humanly and tenderly growled I.

Dead? No. Fainted? No. Even resting? No. He had gone foraging, had captured a log of pine wood, had converted it into a battering ram, and was again storming the castle, with fair prospect, if not of success, at least of the destruction of the outer walls of varnish and the disfigurement of the inner wall of beautiful but determined wood.

"This is *too* much!" springing to the floor with emphasis. "I *will* do something."

"Hush—sh," came from the slowly opened door, through which edged a tall, spare figure, dimly descried in the firelight, turban on, a weighty bucket in hand. "I'd a come before, *but* I couldn't. Sorry to come *through* your room, but this gable winder of yourn looks right over the steps," and, unhurried and relentless as fate, Maria moved across the floor to the "gable winder."

Reaching it, she put down the cumbersome bucket, opened the sash slowly and noiselessly, carefully reconnoitred, drew back with a nod of satisfaction, and stooped for her weapon.

It was of no use to struggle. I laughed again, but in a smothered sort of way, and gasped, "Good gracious, Maria, why do you waste that water? He's drenched to the skin already. Not a dry thread can he have on him—he has been capering round in this deluge for an hour."

Maria was not to be diverted from her purpose by any frivolous talk. The bucket rose—the bucket rested on the window ledge—the turbaned

head reconnoitred once again—the bucket tilted
—tilted more—emptied with a swash.

I sat up to listen.

A howl. An objurgation. Another howl.
Some stamping. A few words of vigorous Saxon.
A disorderly retreat.

The sash was closed, the curtains re-drawn. "I
thought that kitchen fire never *would* burn,"
Maria was saying, as she marched back with the
air of a victor, "and that that there tea-kittle
never *would* bile—but it *did!*" She softly
opened the door. "I hope, Miss Dickinson,
you'll sleep sound *now* till morning," and as she
was shutting it, added, in a stage aside, "I said
I'd like to see him!" and was gone.

It is safe to say the *entire* of that household
"slept sound" till morning, and sitting down to
contemplate our nocturnal visitor through the
dispassionate light of memory, and in the illu-
minating power of broad day, we came to the
unanimous decision that his like we never had
seen, and hoped never to see more.

XXXV.

There is no such thing as unmitigated disaster.
The man was responsible for a deal of righteous
and some unrighteous wrath, a hideous night, a

damaged door, a ruptured engagement with consequent loss of fee ; but he compelled a holiday of a regular working day, and so out of its very surprise gave me a pleasure, and through *that* pleasure I fell heir unto two of the most unalloyed delights of all my life—the sight of the sea under a cloudless sky, after a long November storm, and my first feast of Christine Nilsson in opera!

If you have listened to a many of fine singers before Nilsson speaks to your soul, so much the better for you ; some gauge has been furnished whereby to measure her, and the measuring is soon done.

> " You meaner beauties of the night,
>   That poorly satisfy our eyes
>   More by your number than your light,
>   You common people of the skies,
>   What are you when the moon shall rise ?"

> " Ye violets that first appear,
>   By your pure purple mantle known
>   Like the proud virgins of the year,
>   As if the spring were all your own,
>   What are you when the rose is blown ?"

> " Ye curious chanters of the wood
>   That warble forth Dame Nature's lays,
>   Thinking your passions understood
>   By your weak accents, what's your praise,
>   When Philomel her voice doth raise ?"

Greater than her singing, which pierces to the heart—greater than her acting, which surpasses Ristori's—is *herself*. The woman's supreme power lies in what permeates voice and action. As she comes down to her audience, moving like a beautiful, untamed thing of the desert, before she sings a note or stirs a gesture, she conquers. She has within the divine fire, and you feel its warmth before you hear its flames or see its glow.

XXXVI.

From New England to the District is a good transfer in dismal weather; though, to tell truth, summer or winter, I *always* like to come into Washington. Its steady growth in beauty is a delight to the eye, and is a fair promise of better things to come. When, rolling over the finest pavements in America, I remember the dust heaps or sloughs of mud that, but a few years ago, served for streets, and mark the stately buildings everywhere taking the place of scarecrow shanties, I grow a faith even in that latter-day miracle, the completion of the Capitol.

Indeed, since it has at last emancipated itself from the tyranny of its ancient hotels, and has had the audacity to set over against Willard's that delight of an inn the Arlington, I hold to unlimited belief in its capacity to do any thing.

My last experience, a good many years ago, of the palatial mansion at Fourteenth Street and Pennsylvania Avenue, consisted of a climb—elevators being regarded as impudent interlopers—up five flights of stairs, the possession of a room adorned by three broken window panes, a disabled bell, a ragged carpet, one chair with a broken back, one chair with a rheumatic leg, a washstand not to be depended upon without due watchfulness and *propping*, and a bed that must have been an accurate copy of some one of the beds inquisitorial.

For which luxuries I was permitted to pay the same sum as though I held possession of " a parlor chamber, second floor, front."

To make amends for the isolation to which I was consigned by the speechless bell, and to add cheer to my already attractive apartment, some frisky visitors who have a proverbial *penchant* for rags and dilapidation, proceeded to disport themselves in my domain.

Out of sleep did they summon me. The fire in the contracted grate having asphyxiated, and the night being cold, a change of blankets was a matter to be felt. I felt it. Put out a hand to rearrange the covering. Re-arranged it. Was falling asleep once more, was wakened by a vigorous tug that opened my eyes very wide indeed, and that stirred nerves and wrath together, the first being soothed, and the last receiving augmentation as, in place of a burglar, a squeal and a squeak, and the wabbling of feet revealed the quality of my uninvited callers.

Complaints, and the Arlington, and Time—that sure ender, in some shape, of *all* abuses—have at last amended even this huge nuisance.

A nuisance, in spite of its enormities, dear to the memories of all those who knew it, and its crowds, its sights and sounds, through the tremendous days of the **war**.

XXXVII.

I wish Washington would speak out in a good vigorous way, what I have heard said quietly whenever I have been there—a protest against the annual howl of the outside papers and people about the "female clerks," their sins of omission and commission, and the total depravity of which their appointments stand as indices.

There seems to be a wide-spread impression that

these clerks are all young, handsome, and indolent, that the places filled by them are silken sinecures, and that the pay received is one to allow gilded splendor of abode and dress to its fortunate receiver.

As far as my observation has extended, and it has not been limited, there must be some cracking of ingenuity, or attenuation of comfort by these gay and ease-loving damsels, to "make both ends meet."

Sensible, self-respecting, and industrious girls; tired and sorrowful-looking women, some widows, many of them with children clinging about their knees.

Out of fifty-five women picked at random into whose estate I questioned, I found but eight who were not only their own providers, but the solitary stay of one or more helpless lives.

Many of these are the widows and orphans of men dead in battle.

"That is no reason," say some of these papers and people, "why the government departments should be converted into dispensaries for their needs." No; but it is an added reason why women who are *not* paupers, who honestly earn every penny they receive, should be freed from indecent slander by the lips of persons who know nothing about them, save that they have been left stripped and desolate for the public weal.

Also it would be well for sapient reasoners, who demonstrate that a woman ought not to be engaged by the government, simply because she is a *woman* and in want of work, at the same time to make clear that *being* engaged she ought not to be paid as a *woman* but as a *worker*. Her capacity and not her sex should be the criterion of her compensation.

I know in these departments of girls and women who are doing the like work as that done by men, equally well, in some cases better, they being paid from six hundred to nine hundred dollars a year—the men receiving from twelve hundred to three thousand dollars.

I can put my finger on one woman who is at the head of a department in which are collected papers and books in manuscript by thousands, upon any one of which, at a moment's notice, she can place her hand. From all parts of the building men come to her for information. She has the supervision of two rooms and of sixty girls. She *earns* three thousand dollars; she is *paid* nine hundred dollars a year.

For her tact, skill, executive ability, business knowledge and training, this woman gains no more than the girl who sorts and cuts currency in the next room.

A young girl of whom I know, a skilled linguist, who has state papers to translate, often in such numbers as to compel her to write over-hours and at home, not long since was called to the desk of a young man to straighten out the work he had hopelessly tangled, and did the difficult task to perfection. Incompetency, idleness, favoritism, and man secured two thousand dollars a year; brains, culture, hard work and woman were paid with nine hundred.

Such women as these carry sufficient weight without the addition of the monstrous accusation that their presence is the proof of immorality in the public departments.

People make light estimate of the purity they profess to hold an essential attribute of woman, or they confess for her an awful state of destitution when they so readily concede, without investigation, that she will sell herself, body and soul, for six hundred dollars a year.

For the others, if there be any others, I do not see how the cause of morality is to be damaged by their earning of some honest wage for honest work, nor how that of virtue is to be served by dismissal and consignment to the results of idleness and want.

And if any one says, as many are addicted to saying, that by their contact other women are insulted and contaminated, I answer that I cannot see how these others can be hurt by sight and sound of questionable women, more than by the presence and association of the *un*questionable men who are responsible for *their* appointments—men who are not expected to resign their authority nor to renounce their honors and emoluments, and about whom, in this connection at least, people do not feel called upon to express an opinion.

There is a homely but wholesome proverb concerning the sex of geese and "sauce" for the same, that I would commend to the consideration of some inconsistent and over-nice censors of public and private morals.

XXXVIII.

Also, it will apply, equally well, to *work*, its honors and compensations.

I remember looking at a certain statue, mounted at the Capital and remarking, " As it stands it is a monument to the incompetency of one woman and the folly of some men."

One of the men who had voted for the appropriation that put it there answered, "You are doing what you accuse men of doing—abusing your sex."

"How so?" said I. "Is it the foolish men, or the incompetent woman, or the awkward statue that is the sex abused? I have been expressing my opinion of all of these."

"I mean the young lady who made *it*. How can you, who profess to be a friend to your sex, be so harsh to it and its work?" he answered.

"As far as I know," said I, "my sex did not make that statue; I am sure that even of Americans Miss Hosmer did not, nor Miss Whitney, nor Miss Gibson, nor yet the sum total of the millions of other women known and unknown to fame.

"Concerning its being the work of a woman I no more condemn *my* sex by saying it is a failure, than I condemn *your* sex by saying that *that* statue," pointing to a monstrosity, "or that *that* picture," indicating a daub, each bits of masculine handicraft, "is as hideous as it ought to be beautiful to be allowed space in this Rotunda."

"Oh," cried another of the chivalric and honorable gentlemen, "I am too gallant to measure a woman's work in that way. I must like and praise the work because it is done by a lady."

"'Gallant'? That is what *you* call it? To my mind the praise of a woman's work, *because* it is a woman's, is an insult."

An hour later I was listening to a speech that Knott of Kentucky was making on the floor of the House—a vulgar, ribald speech, almost every member was out of his seat, crowded about him. The Speaker leaned back in his chair, with idle gavel, while these dignified Representatives shouted and roared, and poked one another in the ribs, and then roared and shouted again over the disgusting display, the two *gallant gentlemen* of the past controversy being specially conspicuous for their almost frantic delight, especially when Knott, in discoursing of some law-abiding citizens, who desired to be represented by ballot as well as by taxes, told of these "damsells who wish the right to smoke, chew, swear, drink cocktails, and ride astraddle."

"Gentlemen," thought I, as I watched, "a little less adulation of the 'sex,' if you please, and a little more respect for *woman*."

XXXIX.

Since I desired to think well of my brethren, I was glad to find myself in the evening at the house of that noblest of men and finest of gentlemen, Charles Sumner, who, among other right speakings, always had the courage to tell the truth in behalf of art without consideration of favoritism in men, or sex in women. If Congress had delegated to him the task of ornamenting the Capitol, it could boast a display of *fine* arts indeed.

His house was too small for the treasures he had collected. The hall, on the one hand opening into the drawing-room, on the other to the library and dining-room, and the stairway of black walnut were papered by rare engravings.

Below, the rooms, connected by folding doors, had the expansive effect of one noble apartment. At the right, the drawing-room, showing a lovely Wilton carpet, its chief color an exquisite blue, the curtains and hangings a delicious amber. The pictures, masterpieces, all save one—a freak of his—the chromo of Whittier's "Barefoot Boy." The china, carrying an aroma of palaces, of great value and wonderful beauty.

On one side, the library-doors crowded with engravings of horses and horses' heads. "I never owned a horse," said he, "but here is my stable. Who can equal it?" The other side was covered with likenesses of the most famous gateways and doorways, ancient and modern.

The walls and mantle packed with curious and beautiful bronzes and paintings, even the floor about the walls, supporting pictures that else could find no resting-place. Indeed the room was so overcrowded with beauty as to lose beauty, but the dining-room was perfection, the colors so rich as to be fruity, a Turkish table-cover, wonderful glass and china, and carved things and superb paintings all in absolute harmony.

His study, his "den" as he called it, always interested me, as it must have interested any one who had the happiness to enter it, more than any other room in the house. At the head of the stairway, on the second floor, adjoining his sleeping-room, heaped and jammed with books and papers, on tables, shelves, chairs, the floor itself with scarce space for one to turn. Here he really lived, and you, who looked at it, realized what a hard worker was its master.

Here he had gathered the rarest collection of

framed engravings in America, the careful accumulation of a lifetime. In this country no one else owned such portraits and such proofs, many of them carrying the autographs of both painter and engraver.

To two of these he called my close attention. One, a delicate high-bred face, that of a German noble and patriot who long ago was in prison, condemned to die; the other, that of the wife who, with great skill and through much suffering, rescued him—a strong, homely, heroic face was hers. He went up to it, and looking at it in an indescribable way, said, "I like to have her here. I like to look at her, to remember how brave and strong and unselfish she was, of what she was to him. What a friend! what a friend! Ah, how much more than beauty, or even genius, is *character*."

It was said as though he were thinking aloud, rather than speaking to any one, and with an indrawn, unconscious sigh that pierced like a knife.

When I went away I felt as I always felt, since first, an overgrown school-girl, I beheld him, and shall always feel when I think of him, as though I had been breathing the air of the mountain top, and had heard a voice from the skies.

Well I know, if it was rest he needed, he has gained it. If nobler work, that he has found it, with quickened and immortal powers.

XL.

I often hear people surmise that a Washington audience must be one specially difficult to please. On the contrary, it hears so much bad speaking as to have grown *tolerant* of bad speaking, and knows how to appreciate and make much of the good.

A little country town that listens to about three "domonstrations" a year, even Demosthenes would fail to satisfy.

"I liked him very well," said to me one of these village magnates, speaking of Mr. Beecher, who had shone upon his community the week previous; "yes, I liked him very well, but he wasn't so *energetic* as I expected to find him."

He was own cousin, I suspect, to a man against whom I stumbled a few days later, who was complaining that "Mark Twain had been a great disappointment to him."

"Incredible," objected I.

"Oh yes; he was," asseverated the man.

"He was neither so solid nor so serious-minded as I had supposed."

And *he* must have been twin-brother to a woman whose orbit I one day touched in travelling to Cleveland.

"I couldn't help laughing out loud," I was saying to the friend beside me to whom I was narrating some absurdity, when this woman turned, skewered me with her sepulchral eye, and demanded, "Laugh? Did I hear you say you *laughed?* Why, I thought you never smiled. How can you pretend to be in earnest, in this world of sin and sorrow, and yet *laugh?*"

"I beg your pardon, madam," said I. "I do not at all doubt if I could live for a reasonable length of time under your wholesome influence, I would be cured of such frivolity."

She ought to be transferred to the congenial soil of ——. You can guess the town.

It I reached at six P.M., found the inn burned, and was carried, protesting, to the house of one of the college dons, "where," I was assured, I should "have all the *freedom* as well as all the comforts of a hotel."

Supper was on the table. Supper I wanted

none, but was desired to sit at the board, and so heard what I had never before heard, a grace before meat, of seven minutes in length. The meat being eaten, I listened to what I had never before listened—abbreviated or lengthy—thanks returned after meat.

Having talked for a while, vanished to my room, and returned in battle array for the evening, I halted in the dining-room for a cup of coffee and raw egg, small private flask in hand.

A suspicious glance. An ominous silence. Then the query,

"Does that flask hold alcoholic stimulant—brandy perhaps, or wine?"

Inwardly chattering, but outwardly bold, since I knew I *couldn't* swallow the raw egg without the sherry, I strove to placate my formidable host with a feeble joke.

"If you please, sir, it is not *very* wicked—nothing worse than essence of grape."

"Ah," said the great man, relaxing, "essence of grape? Very well, very well. I feared it was wine or some kindred abomination," and that settled I was allowed to swallow my coffee and egg *and* essence of grape, but not until mine host had spared me the trouble of silent or private thankfulness by the kindly intervention of a lengthy grace spoken in my behalf.

Went to the hall in a subdued frame of mind, meditating whether it would not be advisable to omit the mild provocatives to laughter that here and there cropped out on the surface of an otherwise serious discourse, and was sure of the right path when not the President of the Student's Lecture Association, but the "Presiding Officer of the Meeting," in place of an introduction, offered a prayer of twenty-seven minutes as marked by the clock ticking in full view, in the course of which he besought that "this young woman might be brought to see that no temporal prosperity, nor even the accomplishment of seeming good, justified her in an open defiance of the ordinances of God, and the divinely appointed sphere of her sex," whatever that may mean.

The iniquitous show of the evening ended, its pernicious effects were removed from everybody's memory by another petition, and the singing of Old Hundred dismally out of time and tune.

When I reached home I was in no mood for religious exercises, a fact probably patent to my host, for I had grace said, in my behalf, over my supper and thanks returned when I had completed the demolition of the viands set before me, after which I was summoned, willy nilly, to family prayers, and gained my room in a frame of mind that boded ill to my furniture.

Improved the next day, when, tired and but half rested, I was summoned from refreshing slumber to appear by candle-light at morning prayers, a summons which I neglected, and turned my burning head for "a little more sleep," but was speedily cured of the delusion that I should enjoy any by the piping of a small voice at my door to the effect that "Pa wishes to know if you are not ready?"

"No, my dear," called I in return, "not near ready. Ask him not to wait for me."

Patter, patter of small feet *down* the stairs. Tramp, tramp of large feet *up* the stairs, through the hall. Halt at the door. Summons. Proclamation: "You will greatly oblige us if you will come down soon as possible. It is a rule from which I *never* deviate, to have every member of my household, unless prostrated by sickness, at family prayers."

"Mercifully, I am *not* a member of your household," mumbled I, but was too wrathy to again find oblivion, and when in course of time I appeared below stairs, lo, the assembled family portentously frowning and the Christian (?) services were awaiting me. After which we had grace, breakfast and thanks, and I went my way to the cars with the distinct impression that I had seen a deal of desecration of sacred things.

Likewise it struck me that it would be well if some people would allow other people the privilege of obeying the scriptural injunction of working out one's *own* salvation.

XLI.

My consolation was found in posting into Chicago, as I always do, if I am within a Saturday night's ride of it, to hear Robert Collyer.

To sit and listen to him, to sit and look at him while you listen to the great heart beating through his words, is to sit in a June sunshine and enjoy the peace of God.

He is like the sea, inspiring to great thought, great feeling, great resolve, yet widening to stillness and calm.

The fret and fever of toil, the impatience for results, the eagerness to gather before the seed is fairly planted, the demand for the end from the beginning one by one die out in you, and you are content to do whatsoever your hand finds to do with your *might*, and leave results to God.

It is well for those who believe that perfection consists in absolute ignorance of life and its experiences to heed him : "I pray not that thou shouldst take them out of the world, but that thou shouldst keep them from the evil." We are here, says this clear voice, to struggle with winds and tides, and ofttimes bear some buffetings and suffer their results, since we are here to be *educated*, and education results from struggle.

It is a good thing for selfish or idle people to hear his trumpet-call to the field where all brave souls and true have battle to wage, in one sort or another, for the right. And it is even better for those who think *not* that "God is a good worker, but loves to be helped," but that *they* must do all his work for Him, or perdition will ensue, to take a sense of the broad, steady, even, unfretted, and unfretting power this man brings to his labor.

As I listened to him that day there came to me the fragment of a verse, seen somewhere, and almost forgotten :

> "But while the helping hand, the guiding brain
>   Are fully wrought,
> And while the tears that fall for others' pain
>   Are seeds of thought—
> Leave to a deeper love the tears of care
>   Thou canst not dry;
> Be tranquil. To tranquillity add prayer,
>   But no vain sigh.
> Strength always grappling with all human woes
>   Soon loses breath;
> But strength requickened by divine repose
>   Endures till death.

From church, to dinner in that dear home of his which has the mellow richness of ripe October, with the blessed "mother" and the grand good children, and a hospitality reaching both body and soul—a hospitality that rests and refreshes, reposes and warms.

After dinner came in that jewel of a girl Kate Field. She was taking lessons in western distances and experiences, and we compared notes upon these and kindred affairs, and at parting I wished her God speed with my heart, if my lips failed to gush over her. She is so full of energy and will, so determined to succeed spite of slight frame and protesting nerves and muscles, so ambitious of noble work and place in defiance of fatigue and obstacles, and it is all so plainly marked on her!

Witty, pungent, concise of speech, abrupt of manner, hating shams with a royal hatred.

With beautiful brown eyes that penetrate deep while they reveal depths, and firm mouth that dominates the delicate face and seems to say to it, and to any wearying and weakness that lie behind it: Advance! you have your work to do, your plan set to accomplish; do and accomplish them.

In the afternoon along happened Frederick Douglass, delighting our eyes by the sight of his leonine head and majestic presence, and our ears by his rich and eloquent talk.

He has a "gift" that way! There be those who are rare talkers and yet no speech-makers, and there be orators who are any thing but successful conversationalists, but fortune has here duplicated her gifts.

When you listen to his fiery denunciations and impassioned appeals from the platform, you gather no conception of the wit, the observation, the satire, the pathos, the quaintness that fill his familiar discourse. What store of anecdote, what fund of humor has he not gathered from the knowledge and discipline of life!

And *what* a life!

The afternoon slipped away, all too quickly, and, like all things, good and bad, found an end, but, unlike most good things, an end satisfactory, for when evening came, and supper, wasn't there " a pretty dish to set before a king!" Somebody with more melody in him than all the throats of all the birds could sing: Bret Harte, who was halting at Chicago in his flitting from the Pacific to the Atlantic Sea.

He is *satisfying*—that is the word for him. One thinks all sorts of thoughts about men and women who have accomplished wonders of some kind, and are disappointed at sight. Not so here. You say *this* is the man to have written those stories and sketches full of pathos and power.

In manner he is very quiet. As you watch him you see he knows, as genius always knows, in a steady unpretentious fashion, its own worth. He says rare things in a clear rich voice, and he laughs a mellow sort of laugh that is yet not gay. The man has looked at life and *knows* it, and has carried some of its burthens. That is plain to be seen.

Watching him, there came to my remembrance a critique published in a wise Eastern magazine:

"We suppose that women would not generally find his stories amusing or touching. . . . He does not touch any of the phases of vice or virtue which seem to touch women. We think it probable that none but a man would care for the portrait of such a gambler as Mr. John Oakhurst, or would discover the cunning touches with which it is done in its blended shades of good and evil, and a man only could relish the rude pathos of Tennessee's partner, and of those poor, bewildered sinful souls, the Duchess and Mother Shipton."

Remembering, I laughed to myself softly as I thought of how —— cried over the "Luck," and of how long —— sat still by that tombstone that was the "deuce of clubs," and —— found an eloquence surpassing the music of Amphion's lyre in the speech of "Tennessee's Pardner," and —— night after night took the whole motly company to bed with her, thrusting them under her pillow, that she might again and again feast with them before she drank her morning coffee. And if these were so drawn by their "unlikes," what shall be said of the throng of nameless women who, I *know*, have read these pages with eager eyes and blistered them with tears.

With reason. For here is a great pitiful heart that is not alone generous to his own sex, but is *just* to both men and women.

He has the courage to preach a gospel of equality. "Kentuck," dirty and disreputable, drifts away to the unknown sea holding the innocent baby in his arms, and the " Duchess" dies in the embrace and pillowed upon the breast of a girl as ignorant of harm as the blessed little one.

And see what those outcasts were capable of doing—Miggles for Jim, the Duchess and Mother Shipton for Piney, Sandy's cast-off mistress for her son.

And *what* a lesson in the Idyl! This pure girl taking to her breast the sin-stricken one, adopting her boy, abandoning the man who rightly belongs to another.

Not much of orthodox society plan here!

She should have cried to the woman, "I am holier than thou," refused to work good for the child through his mother's sin-bought gold, left him to be branded with her shame till he lost it in his own—in prison or on the gallows.

And have married Sandy to regenerate him.

Mr. Harte! Mr. Harte! you are an iconoclast. Where did you find such ideas? Are you in polite society? and who is your pastor? I am afraid you have had no better teaching than the Sermon on the Mount, and no better teacher than our blessed Lord.

Well, I am glad to remember that day and its companions, and that they and it belong at Chicago—Chicago always seeming to me to have the actual personality of a human being of whom one can be fond.

XLII.

Did I know it before the fire? Yes, and fell in love with it, and have had a tenderer feeling for it ever since it underwent that fiery baptism.

Did I see it burn? No. But had my sorrowful gaze at it presently thereafter. Let me see—somewhere there is a letter I wrote on the spot. Yes, here it is. You can read it, while I look at these Illinois prairies. No matter about the first of it—'tis a home letter and holds personal affairs—there—*that* is the place to begin:

I drove over to the east side, where I was to speak, in an open carriage, and so contemplated a part of the burnt district, and could not realize that I was in this country, and belonged to this age.

The moon, a crescent moon, had risen and gave its insufficient light to the scene.

Up and down and across, far as the eye could reach, nothing but gray ruins. Not a sidewalk, not a street light, not a living soul in sight for blocks together, not a single pedestrian.

No smoke, no smell of smoke or soot, no *débris* nor waste matter clogging the streets, no gaping windows and doorways, no toppling walls, none of the ordinary marks of fire.

A bit of wall standing here, a chimney base there, and few of these. Queer, grotesque, pathetic-looking shapes, precisely like the views we have of Rome or of some other old-time city fallen not by speedy flames, but wearing decay. It is as though this place had lived and died and left these scant memorials thousands of years ago.

When I came into the church I felt like a ghost that had been wandering through tombs, and indeed the people, though they were certainly living beings, and modern looking of dress and face, did not remove the sense of gloom.

The church is a vast one, and it was very full, and the people—that friendly, helpful Chicago audience—seemed glad to see me; but there was an indescribable *something* in the house that one feels in a dwelling place where some one is lying dead, and though I stuck close to the subject matter of my speech, and they tenaciously followed it, the effort was like that of a sorrowing friend to help those sorely bereaved, in their effort to talk bravely about ordinary and foreign themes, while there is in the hearts of all the woeful consciousness of that open grave.

At last I broke down and spoke of what my heart was full—Chicago and Chicago's loss, and Chicago's heroism and generosity—specially of this last, and its sublime display, when, burned, stripped, homeless, the past wiped out, the future a blank, the present an agony, it took of the first help that reached it from the eager outside world, and sent it to the people of Wisconsin and Michigan in even sorer straits and desolation, and tried to say in *some* shape what Tom Hood has said in *perfect*, shape, that, "the charity that plenty spares to poverty is human and earthly, but it becomes divine and heavenly when suffering gives to want," and to tell them what men and women elsewhere thought of the act and of them. I thought that my time too had come to die, and that we would all be drowned and swept away together. Such crying I never did see in any audience, and yet crying that must have done good to those hot dry eyes and overstrained nerves and brains.

After it was over, still half blind and strangled, I drove back through this city of the silent, and saw not a sign of life save two flitting foot-passengers, and the red light of a solitary street-car creeping along. It startled me, this twenty-year old invention in the midst of seeming antique waste.

The next day I drove over to the north side, where was done the widest work of the fire. It is useless to try to convey to another what you experience in journeying through this region. You can easily tell what your eyes see, but you cannot make another feel what is in your heart.

There is just simply *nothing* to describe. Miles on miles of dreary open space. That is all. There are whole blocks as clean as a threshing-floor, not even a nail left, nor a little heap of ashes of what were once beautiful or pleasant homes. This was the "wooden" part of the town, not poor, the poorest and ugliest part of the city still stands.

There is scarcely a thing that can be called a ruin save the churches, and many of these are literally annihilated. Never before was such awful *cleanness* seen after fire. It is like the open prairie, save that you, standing in its midst, feel instead of the bounding life of the prairie, as though the ground under foot was filled with sadder things than death.

Some idea of the frightful fury of the flames can be had from the heavy pillars of church or public buildings, here and there standing. The outer surface of the solid stone has *boiled* in the furnace heat, run down in streams and hardened on the new face exposed, like petrified jelly.

Here there was nobody — a few sight-seers, strangers—nothing else visible that had life.

Across the river, in the great business section, swarms of men are already at work carting away what rubbish remains, and preparing to build anew, but here things are yet as the fire left them.

We drove till I said to myself, "Now we *must* be at the end, for I can bear no more," and when I reached that point we had but fairly begun.

We paced along over miles and miles till I lost all power of speech, and was dumb when I came back to the home of my dear courageous friends, who tried to laugh at me—and broke down crying. To bed I went at last, only to lie awake through the night. I was not restless, but I felt as though I could *never* go to sleep again.

There is a terrible activity in the mental air of the place. It is penetrated with awful memories, crowded with loss and anguish, and the superhuman struggle of the people for courage and cheerfulness. Every one tries to outvie his or her neighbor in the heroic effort.

One laughs and apologizes for her very fine clothes because they "are all she has," and another is "constantly busy looking after her husband and children by reason of their being scattered in this or that house of friends;" and another, who has a retinue of servants, "finds it jolly living in two rooms, so much less care;" and another who has taken her silken ease in a palace is amused at living in a frame shanty, "it reminds me of '49 and '50;" and this man says, "Oh, *my* loss has been nothing," half a million perhaps, but the man with whom he talks has lost a million, and *he* says, "Well, mine isn't worth mentioning; I'm more lucky than the most: my books are saved;" and another, who went abroad a prince, comes home penniless and congratulates himself that he has had Europe, "*that* is a safe investment nothing can take from me;" and another who had thought his work done begins afresh at fifty, and is sure that he is fortunate in that he "has his credit and energy enough to start anew."

Still the reaction must come.

What I have seen makes me think of the splendid drama played by the old French *noblesse* in the days of the Revolution. It is a sort of intoxication of courage. But when the fine clothes are shabby and there is no money to buy *any* kind, and the break comes after a man has moved mountains to hold his thread of business unbroken, and the bald gaunt face of poverty sits down at many a table, the result will be terrible; even now you hear of invalids and some insane. Think of nearly five hundred little lives breathing an untimely breath, as they passed their whole of earthly experience in some open park or street on that awful Monday night.

The noise of the flames, not the crackling and crashing of stone and timber, but the Voice of the Fire, was, they tell me, like the roar of an angry sea. It deafened people,—and the light was like that of a consuming world. I do not wonder that it seemed to many a soul like "the Judgment Day."

Indeed it was a sort of judgment day, in which the internal Me, the souls of men and women, were laid bare without mask or covering, and the "bed rock" of nature was revealed to the human eye, as it would never else have been seen save by God alone.

And the revelation makes one glad that one lives and belongs to the human kind, and I *must* say it—to the *American* human kind. Robert Collyer testifies, " I did not see a man moaning or a woman crying of *your* stock ; I did not see a single man or woman who was not trying to do something for somebody else more helpless than they were themselves." Still my American brain does not fail to appreciate the fact that it is a man who did more than the most and better than the best who bears this generous testimony with his hearty English tongue.

XLIII.

Life at Chicago was so sad and heroic that even the half week spent there cut me off from the ordinary feeling and action of the world. I was glad to find myself at —— in an atrocious hotel, and so be able to growl over the commonplace disagreeables of time.

And to have a laugh too. It was the first time I had been at ——, and the landlord, wishing to do me honor, was on the steps of his hotel to welcome me with great distinction. Divers high mightinesses had been in order before me, and his tongue had grown so accustomed to titles of rank and dignity as to be unable to compass itself to the small bounds of "miss," and expanded at once into the familiar, "Ah, how de do, colonel? how de do? proud to welcome you to our town;" and then, probably hearing internally an echo of his words, blushed and stopped.

After all I was not greatly flattered. If it had been "general," I might have plumed myself, but "colonel!"—colonels are too plenty. If every colonel of whom I hear or meet was a soldier, the standing army in the country would be a menace to our liberties. Specially throughout the West are they as great in number as they were in San Francisco at the time of John Phœnix's visit, to which number he bears veracious testimony. "The steamboat," he tells us, "was leaving the wharf, and everybody was taking leave of friends—all but Phœnix, who had no friend to bid him farewell. Ashamed of his loneliness as the boat sheered off, he called out in a loud voice, 'Good by, colonel!' and, to his great delight, every man on the wharf took off his hat and shouted, 'Colonel, good-by!'"

And that reminds me of a good story told at —— about the President of the Association and Mr. Phillips. They had tried in vain to secure his services for their last course, and could give no sufficient reason to their people why he should come to places near and about them, and not to them.

Being near them, the President, with a party, went to hear him, and at the close of the lecture fell to cross-questioning him as to his inability or unwillingness to meet their wishes.

"I would not have a good audience," at last said he of the silver tongue.

"How can you say so," queried the President, "when you had such splendid houses before?"

"Not so full last time," objected Mr. Phillips.

"But it rained," expostulated the determined officer. "The night would have hurt *anybody's* house. Our people are more anxious than ever to hear you."

"Can't credit it," objected the great speaker, who probably had his own sufficient reasons for non-compliance with the request. "I have had thrust upon me, from visit to visit, the unmistakable signs of failing popularity."

"But you can't have," protested the President, "because there ain't any failure of that kind. You never began to be so popular."

"Don't tell me," said Mr. Phillips, with a glimmer of smile that *might* have enlightened the befogged ambassador, "when I first stopped at —— the landlord came clear out to the curbstone to meet me, hat to the ground, 'General, I am proud and happy of the honor of welcoming you at last to our town. You will have a worthy reception to-night;' and I was sure of an audience for *that* evening.

"When I came round almost a year later, the landlord stood in the door, hat not visible, 'Colonel, I'm glad to see you again; we'll all be glad to hear you once more;" and I thought, I will have a *full* house if not a *crowd* to-night.

"*Last* year, stopping for the third time, there was no landlord on the pavement, none in the doorway, and when I came to the office to register my name, there he stood, hat on the back of his head, too precariously planted to allow of more than a feeble nod as he called, ' Ah, how de do, captain? Here, Jim, take the captain's bag up to No. 39.' I knew then I'd have a poor house *that* night, and I *did*. You say it was the rain, but the landlord was a popular barometer, and I'll take his warning. If I go this time it will be to find that I am only a high private, with consequent effect on the ' drawing power,' and I'll stay away accordingly."

And spite of entreaties *that* was all the satisfaction that could be gained from him.

To show that he had no possible vacant evening would have been without avail. A plain demonstration of six nights a week for the next six months is no obstacle to an association that has fixed its desires on some particular speaker. " I don't doubt Gough could come well enough if he would," complained a Y. M. C. A. secretary to me one day. " He don't *want* to come."

" To my certain knowledge," answered I, " Mr. Gough has at least three times more invitations every season, at his own price, than he is able to fill."

" Oh, he could come to us if he tried hard enough," growled the disappointed secretary, before whose vision rose the crammed hall Gough *always* draws. "We're only one place more, and we've been trying to get him for the last three years."

"So a thousand other places can say," I contended.

"Oh, well, he could squeeze us in if we could only make him think so. Can't you speak a word for us when you see him?"

"Yes," said I, "I will; and at the same time suggest to him that he have the calendar amended and eight evenings counted to a week."

XLIV.

And the next day, sat ruminating in the cars upon the feasibility of this project, when my ponderings were rudely jostled by reason of the engine plunging into the rear car of a freight train and jerking us all from the track.

"Nobody hurt."

But as the cars bumped over the ties and swayed to a threatened overthrow, I took a fresh sense of the stupidity or recklessness that continues to expose thousands of lives to the horror of slow auto-da-fé's by the crude and senseless methods of heating the cars.

Old traveller as I am, much exposed and little given to fear, I never sit down in that champion tinder-box—a car—in the midst of its upholstery, its dry highly seasoned woods steeped in oil and varnish, and look at its *stove* without a momentary shudder.

It does not need an awful disaster to produce a doubly horrible one. A mishap that would of itself result in nothing worse than a scare and some bruises, is converted through these abominations filled with blazing wood or burning coals into a ghastly tragedy, that is alike awful in itself and a shame to our civilization and its boasted enterprise.

The company that can use hot-air pipes, yet persists in the atrocity of stoves—fire-brands in the midst of kindling-wood—in the face of the well-known fact that almost every great calamity on the rails has been doubled and quadrupled in its results of anguish and death "by the cars taking fire," ought to be held to a *punishable* accountability at the bar of both law and public opinion.

The public, however, from which the "opinion" is to be manufactured, prefer to greedily devour all the ghastly records of the "accident" (? !), indulge in fine irony of private comment to the effect, "Oh, *of course*, nobody's to blame; *the road* will look out for *that!*" and then sit down and wait for a fresh meal of horrors, all the time knowing perfectly well that if each and every one spoke but a single word apiece, but spoke it out loud as to *who* was to blame, "the road" would see to it that no further cause of offence was given in *that* direction.

XLV.

The *next* day I had a lively ride of another kind. The regular train was hours late, but I was consoled by the assurance of a "comfortable car" on the afternoon freight. Which comfortable car proved to be a baggage-car, incredibly filthy, crowded with road employees, emigrants, and vermin, seatless save for boxes, unventilated save by doors, given over to pipes and tobacco-juice. Fortunately, it was a lovely day, spite of the season, and I sat in the doorway dangling my feet outside, and contemplating at intervals, when my nose would allow it, the display of humanity within.

Why will people be so dirty? I often wonder whether it is the habit or affection of long association that makes them cling so tenaciously to that from which some soap and water would separate them? and would a cold-water mission, not for drink but for ablutions, prove any more successful than the manifold temperance crusades.

XLVI.

At the end of that journey I had one of my "experiences" with a lecture association.

There are associations *and* associations.

This was one of the "and's."

Train crept up to the station at 6.55. Nobody there to meet me. Had not been in the place before, the names and grades of the different hotels were consequently unrevealed mysteries.

"Which is the best house?" I inquired of the conductor of an out-going train.

He was not at liberty to designate.

"I can't tell you. We never give any preference. It'd make bad feeling. They are all pretty fair."

Of course I knew that in a town of *that* size there was *one* that *might* be "pretty fair," and certainly the best—and no more.

So I appealed to the ticket-agent, and the telegraph agent, and the baggage-master with, as usual, the like result. Finally fished out my baggage, plunged into an omnibus and went to a hotel—of course the wrong one. Saw *that* before I was fairly within the door. Had a row with the driver before he could be induced to carry me to the right one. Reached it. Waited to see the clerk. Went in pursuit of him. Was grinned at by a group of boors who stood about the bar filling the air with tobacco-smoke and carpeting the floor with tobacco-juice. Ignored them in return. Found the clerk. Found a room. Found no fire.

"Had any of the committee been in?"

"Yes, Mr. Smith had been in in the morning, and I told him he'd better have a room engaged and a fire; but he said you 'might want to stay at a private house, and then the committee would be out a dollar.'"

Not only no fire, but no water in the pitcher, no towels, no coffee, no time to make any: result, eight o'clock before I can wash the grime from my face, comb my ragged hair, and, shabby and hungry, find my way to the hall.

The next season when I halted at —— I was "in time," was settled, was arrayed, was speculating on the audience, and, lamenting the coughs and colds that would be taken by it out of the slush of the streets and the sleet in the air, wondered why none of the committee appeared.

Two *did* appear.

Was I ready?

Yes, I was ready.

Had I rubbers on?

Yes, I had sandals; they were sufficient to cross to the carriage.

Door opened. Black night. Ankle deep slop. Driving storm. No carriage.

Where was the carriage?

They had no carriage. Did I want one?

Yes, I certainly *did* want one, I always wanted one, and the committee always brought one.

Couldn't I do without it?

No, I certainly couldn't do without it. I *preferred* it on *any* night, and I *needed* it on *this* night.

Private conference in the corner.

Exit.

Delay.

Transit to hall.

Speech made.

Desire to return to hotel and supper.

Fresh delay.

"Mr. T. and his wife—Mr. T. is one of our members—took the carriage to go home, thought they'd get there and have it sent back before you got through hand-shaking and were ready."

Carriage arrives. Five young men follow the unhappy speaker into its depths,

The President.

The Vice-President.

The Secretary.

The Treasurer.

Private member.

The Vice-President is put down at *his* door. The distinguished member is put down at *his* door. The carriage veers out of the route to the hotel to put the Secretary down at *his* door. The President and Treasurer come with the speaker to *her* destination, hand her a roll of bills, remount the vehicle, and disappear through the night, supposably to *their* doors.

She—I—the speaker—counts her roll of bills and finds her fee short ten dollars. In the morning sees the Treasurer; regrets but presumes a " probable oversight."

"Not at all. No oversight at all. It's all right."

"How—all right?"

"Certainly; we paid ten dollars for the carriage."

After which there is manifestly no farther call for words, and "I am thankful I have got my hat back from this congregation."

XLVII.

Also, that I am to have the pleasure of travelling onward to a St. Louis hotel, and a St. Louis audience, and of laughing over my stop at —— by the way.

—— is but thirty miles from St. Louis, yet the houses and lands and people are *sights*. Nobody but Dickens could do justice to them; so why attempt it?

He once did so; —— is a place marked in the "Notes." He came to it on a big hunt, and they still show the bit of an inn at which he stopped, and are full of stories of him. My driver was the son of the old hotel-keeper—keeper of the hotel now himself, a yellow-haired, long-legged gawk, who narrated with pride how he blacked Dickens' boots, and how he—Dickens—"went on a glorious old bust. He airn't noways related to you, be he?"

"No," say I, somewhat wondering, the mystery being presently elucidated by the query, "I say, Missus Dickens, whar shell I have your trunk checked onto?"

The hotel had been built on to the old one—the old one now degraded to a hen-house—the most comical place, with deep window-seats, and a ridiculous three-cornered cupboard, and a door set into the room opposite the cupboard also three-cornered (*à la* Dick Deadeye), and furniture that had apparently descended from the ark. Every thing though was scrupulously clean, an unheard-of luxury through the last half week, and I thought to have a night's sleep, but was disappointed.

No one who has not heard and felt these prairie winds can imagine them. Blowing without break over thousands of miles, their sweep is terrific. The day had been sultry as August, and when night fell I thought time had nearly ended. It thundered and lightened and poured as though the sea had broken from the sky, while the wind, as my landlord remarked in the morning, "war enough to blow the dead out of their graves."

"I hope it won't blow you off the rails and inter one," he remarked cheerfully as I went my way to —— a little later.

Not a bad wish for that day and time.

Never saw I such a tempest as broke over the place that afternoon. It was the same that destroyed East St. Louis, but somewhat spent before reaching ——.

At three of the afternoon a darkness fell that was horrible. Not a twilight nor night, but a livid blackness that was awful. The gas burned as in a vault, casting out a circle of rays, but leaving the space about it in profound gloom. The rain fell not in drops, but in sheets, the thunder was like a park of artillery, yet the noise of the wind drowned it, and the lightning was so incessant and brilliant as to furnish light whereby to read, had not its glare blinded one.

It would have been terrible at midsummer, such a storm. In the midst of winter (it snowed that night) there was about it something weird and uncanny that made one shudder—as though the elements had quite broken from all order and control.

XLVIII.

Considering the profound gloom without, perhaps it was not strange the President of the Association was anxious for something lively in the evening.

He was afraid the audience might not like the lecture on "*Jo-ann*," because "we don't read much in this town, and haven't no library, nor yet many books, and there ain't many of us as has more than heard of her."

I suggested that they should take some other lecture that might be a bit *spicy*, and so suit them better.

"No. You're making that *everywhere*, ain't you? Up to Chicago, and down at St. Louis, and all round?"

"Even so," I confessed.

"Well, we are going to have first chop whatever it is, and Jo-*ann* seems to fill the bill."

In spite of his asseveration, however, my friend was not satisfied with the "bill," for he shook his head sadly and slow, and at last ventured, "Nothing brisk in it, eh?"

"Rather the reverse," I was afraid.

"*And* she lived a considerable while ago. I reckon about 1816, wan't it?"

"Nearer five hundred than fifty years," I explained to him.

"Well now! So long ago as that! Really! Well! You see I told you we're not much for reading here. *Do* you mind telling whether Jo-ann was English or French? And where *is* Ark any way?

More surprise at the answer that "Arc" was a "myth," "nowhere"—the "myth" evidently being as great a mystery as the "Ark."

A long pause, during which my literary friend ruminated while stroking his whiskers, and I studied a page of human nature.

"I say."

"Well?"

"It's just a historic piece?"

"No more."

"Well now," brightening hopefully, "don't you think you could liven it up by throwing in a few jolly stories and some jokes, and—and—*that* sort of thing?"

"Have an intermission about the middle of it? Sing a song? or perhaps dance a jig?" I feelingly inquired.

At which with ecstasy the response, "Oh! if you only *would*, Miss Dickinson!"

Well I didn't, and was never bidden back to *that* town.

I did not suppose he could be matched, but I found his mate a fortnight or so later at ——.

Said the very pleasant presiding officer to me

as we wended our way to the hall, "We have engaged Mr. H— to introduce you this evening. Mr. H— is the leading banker here, and very rich, and he wants to go to Congress, and is always more than glad to make a little speech, and—as he does a great deal for our association——"

He smiled and I smiled, and waited for a *sensation*.

And was not disappointed.

Elijah Pogram in the flesh! Just so big and noisy and pretentious, with a vast expanse of shirt-front, white vest, and limp white necktie. Just such a blue swallow-tail with shining buttons. Hair brushed up in just such an "intellectual" manner. Tobacco quid as huge. Hands stuck as determinedly into his breeches pockets.

No sooner did I see him than I knew I was in for it, and I was. After certain little formalities of attitude and quid had been gone through with, thus ran his story:

"Fellow-citizens.

"Ladies—*and*—gentlemen.

"It is my pleasure, my honor *and* my pleasure to be where I am to-night.

"Hem! hem!

"*Any* one might rejoice in such *a* pleasure and *a* honor—hem!

"Ladies and gentlemen, *and* citizens of Elea-noize, *and* fellow-members of this community, the young woman who is to address you to-night has considerable reputation—hem—hem!

"In fact wherever the English language *is* spoken, wherever the American stars and stripes waves, her name is like household words. Listen to her then, and I know, yes, fellow-citizens, I *know* you *will* listen to her since she always addresses herself to the poor, the maimed, the halt, and the blind! You *will* listen to her since she always addresses herself to the ignorant, the downtrodden and the oppressed of every color, clime, and tongue!

"Fellow-citizens of E—leanoize *and* ladies *and* gentlemen, you will now listen to the *o*ration of Miss Anna *E.* Dickinson."

And he was through, mercifully before I had expired of slow strangulation. Being under his very nose in full view of the audience—an audience that did not stir a muscle—I did not dare to laugh and so as nearly choked as was wholesome.

It was worth going to —— to see and to hear. Indeed, there are people and their doings worth crossing a state, not to say a continent, to behold; curiosities not to be observed every day.

I should think there were a good many such in the Missouri legislature at the same time I was at ——. One of the honorable members desired that the hall of the House might be voted to "Miss Dickinson to give her speech on Jonah's Ark there was so much talk about." He supposed "it must be a lecture about *whales*, and might be interesting as well as instructive," and another said *he* would rather hear her on "female agitation" (the two speeches under consideration being "Joan of Arc" and "Woman's Work and Wages"), but as they proposed there should be no tickets, leaving the speaker to pay her own expenses, she concluded that her interest in their mental growth and spiritual welfare did not demand the outlay. She preferred going to that charming town of Independence and a right-minded society instead.

XLIX.

Some parts of Missouri are altogether lovely. About this place, for instance, the farms are immense, perfectly cultivated, trimly hedged instead of fenced, well watered and timbered. The forests alone would make it beautiful. When you have for long journeyed over a prairie country you find even a commonplace surface of land absolutely delightful to the eye by reason of trees. Independence, formerly the starting-point for emigrant trains, stands back from the road, one of the richest and oldest towns in the State, and I looked with pathetic interest at the spot from whence so many thousands and tens of thousands camped and rested and said good-by to all that was behind of home and civilization, and started upon the long journey across the plains, some in hope, some in indifference akin to despair, many and many a one to sooner find a halting-place than that toward which their weary feet tended.

There is as much to sorrow as to rejoice over in this wonderful far Western growth—in more ways than one.

In too many cases the men are reckless fellows who destroy themselves with excesses and drink.

The women live in their cabins (solitary in the midst of great spaces), toil and moil early and late, their own housekeepers, cooks, maids, nurses, drudges. Bearing half a dozen or a dozen children, burying part of them, by and by lying down by their side, leaving space among the living for No. 2 to step into a handsome home and a good time!

Having wearied myself with melancholy reflection, I nearly fell into convulsions over the extraordinary turnout that met my vision as I turned away from the sight of the old emigrant road.

A waggon of wood, the very tires on the wheels of wood in place of iron, the design of the establishment, to speak mildly, unique, the household belongings unique. Perched on these, two tired-looking saffron-hued women, each with a baby in her arms, and eight or ten small tow-heads bobbing about among the afore-mentioned household goods and chattels, as part and parcel of which they seemed to be stored. Two anatomies of oxen leading; two anatomies of men, sallow, long-haired, "jeans" covered men walking alongside.

Somebody asked one of the pioneers whence they came and whither they were bound. To which answer was vouchsafed, "What's that your dad ratted bisniss? We're from North Calini and are going to Kansas if we can ever git out of these yer blamed houses."

L.

I found here as elsewhere in the Western part of the State a plenty of audiences that were "conservative," but delightful people to whom to tell the story of Jeanne d'Arc.

Cultivated and well read, though you would not think it from their external appearance; odd-looking companies, the women with their coats of many colors and many fashions, and the men with their tobacco and their manners—savoring so much of—well! I do not know what—unless it be an equal mixture of courtier and Indian.

I could readily understand why the story was so well liked by them, with its heroic and pathetic central figure, and its tale of a weak and almost crushed people making triumphant headway against a powerful foe.

Not that I heard lament for things past, nor refusal to accept the inevitable present nor things to come. The great body of people here, as the great body of people everywhere, have been *led*. These have been led astray, but they are getting into the right road, and are struggling nobly toward an end that shall be peace and good will.

I was amused at a bit of argumentation to

which I listened on my way from C— to Kansas City.

A fossil and evident "stay-at-home" was dilating to another of like ilk on the divine right of slavery, and the wrongs and sufferings of the slaveholders.

He must have been a foolish man to have spent his living moments in talking about a thing utterly dead.

Opposite him sat a bright-faced one-armed Missourian, who looked as though he had given the boys in blue some hot work, watching and listening with an amused smile as the mummy iterated and reiterated, "God Almighty never meant the damned niggers to be free! No. He *never* did. He never meant it!" and at last breaking out with—

"Well if that's so, he must be a mighty mean sort of God, for the damned niggers got the best of him."

Whereat everybody in the car, native and foreign, broke into a roar.

LI.

The country from Kansas City down to Fort Scott is the "Debatable Land," and from point to point I heard names that made me start as they were called, thinking that if "old John Brown's soul was marching on," it might be hereabouts to look after the fate of his former camping grounds.

And thought of it the more by reason of the companionship of a fellow-passenger—Stringfellow of "Border Ruffian" fame.

A man of medium height, very strongly and muscularly built, small hands and feet, large head, fiery red skin, hair and whiskers white now, once sandy, the whiskers cut short about mouth and chin, giving a hard bristling look to a jaw square to ugliness and a mouth already firm to cruelty. Large perceptive, small reasoning faculties. The nose of a fox. Eyes of a lead blue, the coldest and most sinister I ever met. A look of great power and endurance to the whole man.

I wondered did any ghosts gaze in at him, or touch him as he went by.

He would not have known it.

And yet I don't know—*Legree* was terrified past control by the "voices" that came down the garret stairs in that house of horrors he called his home.

At —— I concluded I was certainly on the

"Border," as my landlord enlivened the proceedings of the day by firing at and almost killing his clerk, over which little unpleasantness nobody appeared at all disturbed. A cheerful country!

It will take at least one generation to forget the lessons of barbarism, and another to learn those of civilization, and these people in common with the rest of Kansas are doing the best that can be done for present and future by their royal support of the best school system in the land.

Of my own experiences what chiefly impressed me at —— was the littleness of the room in which I held forth, and the bigness of the man who had, as expressed by himself, "the honor to preside on this memorable and delightful occasion," a Missouri colonel (every man here is a colonel, a general, or a judge), who stood seven feet "in his stockings."

I was apprehensive for the roof as his head rose upward, and somewhat scared for myself as he planted his feet—feet that were foundations for this height, objects that he regarded with manifest pride as he turned them about for inspection, and informed me there wasn't a pair of ready-made shoes in the State he could "get on."

Also, he wore a shirt of unbleached cotton,

without collar, fresh, yet already creased and tobacco-stained, into the limp front of which was thrust a magnificent diamond of purest water and superb size; and *he* was as kind, and genial, and intelligent as his diamond was bright — an out and out gentleman.

If you wish to see human nature in all manner of curious developments, "go west."

LII.

As to the hotel conditions under which you will study it, at a woeful many of places, ask no report.

For instance, how many and grievous wounds have I carried away from countless inglorious contests at ——! How many times journeying from it to various other points in the State have I enjoyed unmolested possession of an *entire* seat in a crowded car, and been shunned by erst-while eager committee men, who sheered off silently, or tremulously asked, "Is it safe for you to be abroad, so soon, after so violent an attack of *small-pox?*"

There is a great deal to be said in extenuation of some of these hotels; such as the heat, and the sand, and the vermin-ridden wood of which the houses are frequently constructed, and I would defy even a Pennsylvania Quaker housekeeper to make any headway against the *fleas*—fleas not so big and fierce-looking as those of California, but abounding like the locusts of old.

Still there are limits.

Apropos to this agreeable theme, the other day I heard a story, at the expense of this my most merciless persecutor of a house, that I enjoyed. (No, I will not tell you the house nor the town. The town is a Kansas city, and if you travel you will have to go to the city and being there go to the house, since 'tis the best the place affords. Why torment you untimely by knowledge of what is to come?) People of delicate sensibilities who stay at home, and have not a fellow-feeling born of suffering, need not read.

"Yes," this western man was saying to another rough-looking customer, " you may believe it or not, thar he was a walking down the page of the register when I wrote my name. 'We-ell!' said I to the clerk, 'this beats me! I've had gray-backs a swarmin' on me when I was at Libby prison, and I've been eaten of muskeets down to Orleans, and I've had my tussle with fleas and buggers in this country, but dern my skin if this isn't the first time I ever *did* see a bedbug walk down the register to find the number of a man's room afore he'd taken possession of it.'"

If one cannot fall into ecstasies over the hotels, one *can* wax enthusiastic over other matters. The most of these Kansas towns are delightful. The houses tasty, many of them built of the soft light stone that here abounds, giving a substantial and *old* look to infantile settlements. Clean sidewalks, abundant shade, vines and flowers blooming in early season, every thing tidy and busy, cheerful and progressive. Kansas is like Iowa in its population: New England elements, of thrift and energy and cleanliness, and devotion to education predominating.

The country has a steady lift toward the mountains, and some of the marvellous clearness of the high lands beyond inheres in its atmosphere. The sun goes down a golden or crimson glory, with few or no clouds, and the night soon falls. I should think the New England people would miss the dear delight of twilight time and its musings.

I slipped off the train at Leavenworth, abandoned talk and companions for a while, in the midst of this last journey to Colorado to renew acquaintance with the face of some spots, that, after all, I did but find in memory.

When I was first in this place I had hurried past a deal of modern growth to look at the house where the Phillips brothers were, in the early days, shot at their own door, and at various points in the open streets where brave men fought and died to save the land from slavery, and going on from the ground where they had fallen — early martyrs to a cause that ripened five years later— I climbed the rugged side of Pilot Knob to see where they were laid to their final rest. It is the highest land between the Rocky and the Eastern Mountains, a great ridge looming up in these flats, the landmark for many a belated hunter or emigrant train.

Time's obliterating fingers and the "march of improvement," had left no trace of the spots where they had fought and slept, and I pondered through the night, as the train sped away, the pathetic question of poor old "Rip," "Are we then so soon forgotten when we are gone?" and concluded it was well to live one's life from day to day, since there is not only none in the grave, but precious little memory of it, though it be filled by what has eternally forgotten comfort and happiness and personal gain and present pleasure for the welfare of others, or for the honor or love of those who are too busy with their present to remember what has been done or endured or gained by another in a past that dates back but yesterday.

LIII.

I wonder what the people out in the country across which I gazed the next morning think of "fame and future." In all the broad expanse no human habitation met the eye, and yet there were a plenty of human beings. Through this inhospitable land, where stone does not abound, and wood is more than scarce, and storms are awful, the people who are here, from election or necessity — road-workers and the like — have made for themselves "dug outs," which being interpreted signifies they have burrowed holes in the ground, banked these over with the thrown-out earth, turfed the foot-high roof, and so found themselves "at home."

As I looked at these, there came before me another scene: the James River in the summer of '65 and the counterparts of these same hutches

—kennels where our men had taken food and shelter while working on the fortifications, shielding themselves not from cold but *fiery* rain, and I thought that for a little while, at least, I would like to change the view, and see that lovely river and its beautiful banks now that long years of winter storms and summer suns have smoothed away all the scars of war.

But in that case I would have lost the next morning's ride, when, a few hours out of Denver, we clambered through the dusky light to the pilot of the engine for a scud never to be forgotten.

You know what the "pilot" is? No? Well, it is the flat edge, a foot wide, to which the "cowcatcher" is attached, and the crack point for observation of the train. A gorgeous seat! specially when you are so lucky as to be in the good graces of the engineer to the extent of the bestowal of his leather cushion, which is the last and only touch needed to make perfect your iron perch.

There is a wonderful sense of exhilaration in riding after such fashion through still scenes and quiet landscapes. Nothing is before you, nor at your side. The sky for covering, the surface of things "all ow-doors" about you, the great monster choo! choo! chooing! behind you, toiling and moiling like a brawny giant. You, flying through the air without sense of motion save that of delight and ease.

But through *this* country!

The broad swells, dark and cold, like an angry sea spread round us, clearing as we gazed, the air crystalline, the freshness of morning blowing in our faces; the sky!—a slow retreat of darkness on the one hand, a steady advance of soft yet glowing light on the other. Before us the majestic mountain line, taking shade after shade of purple and amethyst as the rising sun struck against and up its seams and cañons.

The clouds, drifted up and down, were blown aside, massed themselves together, sometimes seeming on the ground from which the stately peaks lifted as from a base of fairy land; sometimes, where the sun burnished them, so high and white and shining as to counterfeit snow-clad summits, and leave the watcher in doubt as to which indeed was mountain and which its cloud semblance.

Colors of all sorts revealed themselves on the face of the range—a rock superb in its native hue without the help of air or cloud effect, a deep rich red, Tyrian purple rather, and gradually, beyond the stretch of plain, beyond the first range dense and grand, rose in the air, peak after peak of farther ranges gleaming with the sunrise on unmelting heads of snow.

So we rode for hours, seeing neither fence, nor farm, nor house, nor human being, and at the Junction, a mile outside the city, scrambled back to our "Pallas" car, assumed sublime unconsciousness of rampant hair and grimy hands, and general "towsle," and came into the civilization of a town in civilized shape.

LIV.

About what were the good people of Denver thinking when they planned their delightful city at *right angles!* Nowhere can you stand at doorway or window and get an unbroken view of the magnificent sweep of mountains. Somewhere a hindrance of chimney or spire, or even cottage roof, cuts off the whole marvellous view.

And *what* a view! and what ether through which to gaze at it.

No one who has not seen and felt it can have any idea of this atmosphere—clear, crisp, magnetic. The sky deep in hue as sapphires, often like a dome of lapis-lazuli, the clouds masses of dazzling glory, the air without dimmings of mist or vapor, a transparent medium of light, so white and resplendent as to be actually painful to an eye that is at all tired or weak. (Remedy, goggles, brown and big. Never travel through such a country without them if you would be absurdly hideous and luxuriously comfortable.) There is no use in trying to describe these sun and air effects, one might as well endeavor to grasp them in one's hand and *so* hold and transmit them, as strive to send them to another's vision from the point of a pen.

One afternoon we went out to see the sun set, driving away toward the ridge on the eastern plains, and so moving fell into the line of the sorrowful procession of the grave.

It was all out of place! There are spots a plenty on the face of the earth with which death seems in keeping, and looking at which you say, this ground was made for graves—but not *here*.

And what life had gone before this ending!

The old, old story.

A young girl, beautiful, accomplished, helpless—the daughter of rich and well-bred people in St. Louis. Trusting, betrayed, abandoned, her love accounted unto her for crime, outcast striving in vain to reconquer lost ground, thrust from depth to depth, till in a few years, in sight of these mountains, and on such a bosom of nature, she lies down to her last sleep.

As I looked at sky and mountain and plain—a heavenly glory — and then at the gloomy and contracted confines of her grave, I thought: surely this last must be likeness of her life past; this first, prototype of her life to be.

God knows all: doubtless she has tested and proven *his justice* to be more infinitely tender than the mercies of man. So thought I, turning from the sad companionship and going back to the delightful town.

LIV.

Denver is so charming as to serve as a trap to hold the uninitiated traveller from the wonders beyond. He needs energy to pack his bag and scramble for the "narrow gauge" road running south.

A curiosity in itself is this little road, completed now from Denver to Alamosa, with the intention of pushing it through to the city of Mexico when permission is granted by Mexican authority to lay the rails across Mexican soil—and the money for stock is subscribed.

Let it be recorded as a miracle that this road

has neither asked nor received government aid. It issues no passes, demands in return no unjust favors, and tries to hold its own honestly. The capital so far invested in it is mainly English, and the most agreeable of English people are spreading themselves throughout this region.

An ordinary " compromise " gauge road could never have been accomplished. Its cost would have been too formidable. The width of such an one would be 4 feet $10\frac{1}{2}$ inches, weight of iron 75 lbs. to the yard, length of cars from 50 to 70 feet. Imagine this baby road: 3 feet wide; weight of iron to the yard of rail, 30 lbs.; length of cars, 40 feet.

The right sort of thing where money is scarce, and uninhabited land scanty of travel, and freightage plenty.

The right sort of thing, too, for steep grading and narrow cañons and mountain passes, since these cars can be switched with ease round curves that would swing off any ordinary train to destruction.

The right sort of thing, also for capitalists to study in the way of enterprise and economy, now that people are growing restive under the weight and *width* of the great corporations.

Or, better still, that first-class mechanics would do well to ponder and work from, instead of serving as tools in the hands of "bloated aristocrats." Such a road can be built, as part of this Denver and Rio Grande has been constructed, as a co-operative enterprise, anywhere.

People slip down this D. and R. G. road to reach Colorado Springs and the weird-looking places about it.

The town itself is admirably located for a watering-place, within easy drive of some of the greatest wonders of this strange region, "The Garden of the Gods," "Glen Eyre," "Monument Park," "Cheyenne Cañon," "Manitou Springs." Over against it is a spur thrust out from the second of the great ranges, with Pike's Peak keeping watch over all.

LV.

We went up to look at the face of the Peak and its revealings. Scrambled along a narrow trail for a dozen miles to the Alta Laguna, halted, kindled an enormous fire of fallen trees, supped, stretched ourselves out to sleep, or to lie watching the tall white trees standing in serried ranks along the sides of the mountain, the dark lines of far-off ridges rising against the quiet sky, the sky seemingly nearer, the stars brighter than those looked at in other lands.

Up at 2.30, away, away through timber growing thin, till at five o'clock, eleven thousand feet above the sea, we saw the sun rise, and reached timber line and the end of the trail. Plunged off into space and *to work* over solid masses of broken boulders and granite till at last at eight in the morning we gained the summit.

Can I tell any thing about it?

Not much.

One goes to the top of a mountain for emotions, not descriptions.

Can I make you see it?

Not at all.

At the east the vast stretch of plains, purple like a great sea. To the south-east and south, two long stretches of mountains finished by the stately domes of the Spanish Peaks—one hundred and ten miles away. To the south-west and west, fully a half-dozen stupendous ranges, their imperial heads blazing with snow, valleys lying between, silvery lines of rivers flowing across, and off at the north-west and north, still the mountains, headed by the majestic height of Long's

Peak, one hundred and fifty miles away. The four great points of Long's Peak, Grey's Peak, Pike's Peak, and the Spanish Peaks, making a line from the north-west to the south-east, we standing on one of them, and feeling as though God were very near, and his world, poor and small as we are accustomed to call it, a thing to awe and yet elevate the looker-on to more than a level with the angels.

We prowled to and fro, we gazed and gazed again, we sat here and there on the edge of things, and looked across creation, or straight down sheer precipices of two thousand feet ; we tore ourselves away at the end of three hours, and plunged, plunged, plunged our way back to camping ground and food after thirteen hours of work and fasting, scrambled into saddle, and found ourselves at Manitou at midnight.

LVI.

Mem.—Never climb without a lemon. It costs little. It weighs lightly. It burthens no one even in this thin air. Cut in two and devoured at the right time, it is the most absolute refreshment and the most stinging and staying stimulant a tired climber can ever know.

LVII.

You are weary? You really *want* as well as *need* rest and refreshment? You are sure you won't hanker after the fleshpots of hotels and Saratoga trunks and fal-lals? Well, then, do as we did.

What did we?

Got a pair of good beasties and comfortable vehicle, clambered into it cased in light woollen garments so that neither sunnings nor wettings could trouble us, with substantial hand-bags, a bucket to water the horses; some lunch; some field-glasses, and divers odds and ends by way of baggage—and made for the Twin Lakes and " Derry's."

Rode thirty-three miles the first day. From Colorado Springs to Manitou, up the wild Ute Pass to the beautiful open country beyond; through Hayden's Pass, where on either side the road nature has piled a vast mass of boulders to the height of four hundred feet, as regularly and symmetrically as though done by a mason's hand; across land that was rich and prolific, though we had started at an elevation of six thousand and were unconsciously moving along to an elevation of nine thousand feet, and toward sun-setting turned a mile or so from the line of our travel to see some petrified stumps of trees.

And shall never forget the spot where they stood.

A place-like an enormous basin, the sides gently sloping up to the level brim all around. Short, soft gray grass covering the ground. Timber on the uplifted surrounding edge miles away, each twig and leaf of which stood out soft yet distinct as an ivory painting in one's hand. A sky and air for which I could find no likeness save the " pearly clearness of the Celestial City," the coloring shot through it reflected from the clouds and the sunken sun making a " light that never was on sea or land." The pallid massive stumps, ghostly and cold, of what had been wood ages before the deluge. Not a sound. Not a chirp of cricket, nor stir of twig or leaf, or blade of grass, nor whisper of bird. Not a sight or vestige of existence, human or brute. It was awful, yet filled with enchantment.

We carried its exalted spell till we reached Costello's jolly hospitable ranche, with its queer little rooms lined with canvas and adorned with innumerable copies of illustrated newspapers, its huge open fireplace made of petrified wood, its gorgeous fire, its royal supper, and yet more royal beds of sweet-smelling straw.

Don't you wish you knew Judge and Madame Costello, and that they would let you come to their ranche, and feed you and talk to you, and make you happy, and at departing allow you to capture from the museum on their open veranda some antelope-horns or deer-horns, or horns of Rocky Mountain sheep, mineral specimens or petrified wood?

If you don't, it is because you are a poor benighted mortal, with no knowledge of what you are rejecting.

We meandered away from it with reluctance, though we had before us some long heavenly days of driving across the South Park, and over the Arkansas Divide.

LVIII.

The Arkansas Divide.

Ah!

Early one morning, after an ascent of five miles of steep mountain road, wild, tangled and beautiful, at an elevation of 9475 feet, what a sight burst upon us—the greatest our eyes ever beheld; the finest, probably, they ever will behold in life.

Behind us, noble mountains dwarfed by what was opposite. A descent to the broad lovely valley of the Arkansas, the river fringed with greenery, gleaming in its midst. Over against us the vast lift of the backbone of the continent—the great main range of the Rocky Mountains, its white rock turned to pale pink and warm light amethyst in the sun, its dazzling heads thirteen, fourteen, fifteen thousand feet high, majestic and overwhelming in their proportions rather than beautiful, though with one great peak balanced on either side by lower ones—a single mountain, the most tremendous and at the same time graceful and symmetrical object that ever filled my vision.

LIX.

We drove in face of these for some miles, down the slope of the Divide to the Valley, then straight north, the mountains on one hand, the river on the other, into wild and savage cañons, out of them across wider spaces, finally quitting the river and following up Trout Creek to Derry's ranche and the Twin Lakes—lakes that lie at the base of ranges themselves 9130 feet above the level of the sea, between two and three miles in length, of the same depth—seventy-five feet—almost alike in shape and size, and connected by a narrow yet deep channel.

"Derry's" is a place at which to *stop*, with its hewn logs without and great whole logs for rafters within, its walls and ceilings papered with *Harper's Magazine*, its floors and doors of dressed pine that looks like the most exquisite satin, floors bare save for some bear-skins, its quaint home-made tables and rocking-chairs, its beds of straw on boxes, its big open fireplace and great fire, and its *roof*—a roof made of fruit-cans baked, opened, flattened, lapped one over the other—that no storm can penetrate; yes, and its trout and green peas, and its mistress shrewd as she is kind.

Back of the Twin Lakes among the giants stands Mt. Elbert, whose shoulders we desired to climb but wished to spare our own means of locomotion.

How to do it—for there were no horses at Derry's and Derry's filled the bill.

No; fortunately for us two miles away was the camp of the Marshall scientific party, the learned men absent, and the camp in possession of the unlearned and obliging; otherwise, some of the guides and attendants.

To it we tramped, held a pow-wow with the one left in authority, resulting in *his* appearance early the next morning in company with a scout and six strong, tall, long-legged, intelligent, friendly mules, branded U. S.

Our guide, Standefer by name, was a specimen of frontier growth in full bloom—a man who had lived his life, since as a boy he quitted Texas, among the mountains, hunting or guiding when not engaged in the, to him, far more satisfactory labor of killing Indians. He had fought over the whole face of this great country, had served the Government as scout and spy, was in the first of the Modoc war, and at date was looking after the welfare of science as embodied in the Marshall party.

He was dark as an Indian, with dead-black hair and eyes to match. He knew all that nature would reveal to close scrutiny. Straight as an arrow, hard as iron, tough as leather. Rode at a dead run without touching bridle. Would fire at a bird on the wing and pick up his game as his animal flew by.

Luckily, he could scent the way where trail was

none. Up the first of our ride was a species of one that no eye untrained to such life could find, so dim it was and so little used. Steep—so steep in places as to give you the sensation of being suspended in mid-air ; by and by running into a forest of aspen trees so low and close as to compel you to duck your head until you found it convenient to lie along the neck of your beastie *all* the time, unless you wished to be made a torso. Under foot, stretched at length, the enormous trunks of fallen trees—a path to exhaust an athlete in an hour, but over which our sure-footed mules skipped like grasshoppers.

This timber growth is something amazing, standing green and strong and beautiful at an altitude at which in other lands *all* life is done, and even when it ceases lovely flowers and thick green grass bloom where elsewhere naught is to be seen save deathly glaciers.

We climbed on and on, the mules panting a little, but not seeming to suffer, over one mountain, along the rugged brow of another, to the final ascent, stony and steep, a mass of boulders and broken rocks, and so at last to the top.

Behind us the scene was one to be paralleled by other mountain experiences—but before ?

Looking to the west and north-west it was as though the world were a sea. From this height no plains nor valleys nor open spaces could be seen, just billows stretching beyond billows of these august swells. Heads that stood thirteen thousand feet, below us. Everlasting snows, below us. More than fifty above fourteen thousand feet, thrust up grandly about us; over against us a shining splendor called "Snow Mass," that fairly blinded us as we gazed.

Above all this, heavy clouds began to grow and slowly settled down, making a sombre veil out of which huge uncertain forms loomed awfully grand, and finally closing them from our sight.

On which we fell to the commonplace duty of devouring our lunch with avidity, and the not commonplace delight of rolling off huge boulders and watching them as they fell, finally turning our feet downward. Nobody was eager to mount a mule and ride *off* the cone. So we went our ways, and the animals went theirs peacefully enough before us.

Let a mule go—and he *goes*.

Try to drag him—!

In the evening, on our return, going into the kitchen for some hot water, I found a gracious-mannered, Latin speaking youth who had asked to join our party that morning, "peart as a cricket" after his day's tamp, and diligently cooking our suppers.

He was one of a small army of young men to be found in that country—civil engineers out of work, miners, hunters, intended settlers, nearly always bright and well informed, short of money, not wanting to turn back, in love with this wild life, thinking they have all time before them, and so well content to spend a little of it without care and in glorious health, "squatting" with some family, cooking and making themselves " generally useful "—ready for what may be beyond.

LX.

If there had been no Mt. Lincoln to see, I know not how long we would have staid at Derry's, but to Mt. Lincoln we at last went: back across the Divide and the northern part of the park to Fairplay, Dudley, donkeys, mountain road, mountain top. Lincoln is one mass of silver ore, and we wanted to see a mine " in the sky."

Think of delving fourteen thousand feet above the sea! More than twice the altitude of Washington, with unmelting snows below it, and clouds brushing in and out of it, each storm that touched it causing electricity to pull at the worker's or observer's hair like a human hand. Think of men living and toiling and enjoying themselves at a height where in Europe all life would be suspended!

We watched the miners drilling and blasting, and saw that the men—splendid specimens of physical vigor—who wielded the heavy sledges had to stop and rest for a breath at every two dozen or so of blows, though they seemed to suffer in no other way.

When you stand still or move slowly in this atmosphere, you experience no difficulty of breathing, and do not realize how high and thin it is, till you run or make some exertion; then your heart tries to fly out of your mouth and your lungs work like bellows.

I found *that* on Grey's Peak, where there was plenty of "footing it" to be done—and oh! wouldn't I like to do it over, dinner at Georgetown with dear old "Commodore Decatur," known and loved of venturesome travellers— Charley Utter and all!

LXI.

Charley Utter is a hunter and guide, and maybe you are not to be accounted one of the lucky ones if you get *him* to lead the way!

I had been up Grey's Peak and many another peak in the daylight, but wished to journey up it in the night, and watch the sun rise from its awful height, and to Charley Utter's we went to find a companion and guide.

How little Eastern people know of these hunters and mountaineers! They imagine a yelling, drinking, fighting, half-Indian crew. Charley will serve as a specimen of the reality.

Short and slight, with long blonde curling hair, blue eyes that look at you fearlessly and through you searchingly, a wide-brimmed slouch hat, moccasins and Indian leggins, a red flannel shirt with embroidered collar and cuffs, a short loose coat, a broad belt with bowie knife, pistols, a tomahawk stuck into it.

There he is.

Chary of speech, soft-voiced, abstemious of habit, gentle-mannered, thoughtful of every one, tender-hearted, his eyes filled with nature, his soul feeling it, and showing itself through quaint broken sentences, delighting in talk that touches the heart of things, or that concerns the lives of the great ones of the earth, over which he has pored and dreamed by his camp fires.

There he is too.

We found him *not* in his pretty cottage home—and thereby hangs a tale worth the telling.

There came to Georgetown a professional man with his wife, poor, broken in health, houses scarce and rent high. Out of his cottage turned Charley, making it over to his neighbor from afar, rent free, and himself pre-empting an old cabin consisting of one big room proceeded to *camp* for the summer.

What a picture we found the room, with the sloping roof, log walls and shining white floor, one corner serving as kitchen, one as dining-room, and a very pretty dining-room too ; the third given over to a picturesque bed and shelves built into the walls, from which shone glimpses of lace and Indian embroidery adorning bright-hued garments ; a charming bit of drawing-room revealed in the fourth, with its square of velvet carpet, its table loaded with books, its cosy chairs and pretty ornaments, the walls hung with pistols, rifles, tomahawks, bows and arrows, interspersed with pictures. Presiding over all, Mrs. Utter, a beautiful dark girl, with brilliant yet soft color, large lovely brown eyes, a mass of rich black hair falling over her shoulders, a velvet jacket and purple skirt covering her: twenty-two, and married for seven years!

LXII.

Well, Charley took us in hand, marshalled us out of Georgetown and up to timber line and supper, with a few hours' sleep following, and had us in our saddles at two of the morning.

What a ride! The clouds had broken away, and the moon, full and splendid, was shining overhead, the gauziest of vapors making about it an enormous circle of delicate rainbow tints. The ground was white with snow, fresh as though newly fallen on the rough broken granite, the unevennesses beneath making its frozen surface far more glitteringly beautiful than it could have been on level ground. The night was still as great heights, and bitter cold, and absolute solitude could make it.

We circled the dome of one and another mountain, and journeyed past the harsh wall of a third, its lines and gorges brought into bold relief by their fleecy covering; these all past, their huge bulks turning to insignificant cones below us, we were fairly out on the bleak, white, frozen height toward whose top our mules were slowly climbing, slipping and stopping for breath, yet sure of foot as Fate itself, in the end.

No Christmas morning below was ever half so cold as we found that top, and the wind would have blown our skins off had we not flattened ourselves on the inhospitable peak that would yield us no suggestion of shelter. Here, numb yet eager, we gazed at the sky overhead, the moon, the ghostly outlines of near mountains, and with infinite anxiety at the shadowy space of the eastern sky.

Slowly the crimson ball lifted itself above the long black line of the horizon.

Under it — to the east — the plains stretched away a deep misty blue, cut by the glittering golden line of the Platte. Northward the ragged lines of the Boulder Hills, their purple edges, jagged like enormous saws, revealed against an amber sky. Off at the south and west, first one then another and another, and yet another, vast, solemn, majestic, range after range of the mountains of eternal snow.

A superhuman revealing.

First darkness. Then shadows that shift—are there and not there. Presently out of these, here and there a peak defined, followed in a breath by the long line, white with a sort of preternatural glory, lying up against the sky like a splendor of clouds, but showing the clear space *behind* them, their enormous bulks gradually coming out through the vanishing darkness below.

Away behind us stood the vast pile of Pike's Peak, a mass of glowing yet delicate violet, balanced by the gigantic line of mountains at the west, among them the Mount of the Holy Cross, on whose black face a chasm of fifteen hundred feet held snow white and clear, in the shape of the divine ignominy. Still beyond this, in what seemed else all open space, the spirit-like outline of a mountain that looked so stupendous and dark as to make one shiver as one gazed. I watched and watched for long before discovering it to be the *shadow* of Grey's Peak on which we stood.

Conceive a shadow two hundred miles long, cast over against the sky, in seeming like a solid mountain, *behind* others so tremendous as to be overwhelming!

It was like the dawn of creation to watch. It was as though the Almighty were calling the muster-roll of form, and peak after peak answering in turn and taking its place, as though it had never been taken before but were to be held now forever.

If it had "staid just so," *we* would probably have staid till we were petrified or blown away. Fortunately for overwrought emotions and frozen bodies it *didn't*, so that at last we were satisfied to take to our feet and plunge downward a half dozen miles to the Kelso cabin and a breakfast that disappeared as though fallen upon by wolves, after which we deigned to mount our mules and pace away in a respectable and comfortably commonplace state of mind.

LXIII.

That would have been our last climb for the summer had we not been taken in hand by the Hayden party, thereby gaining the experience and memory of Long's Peak, and the companionship through a few days of men who ought to be immortal if superhuman perseverance and courage are guarantees of immortality.

What a pair of heads had that party! Hayden, tall, slender, with soft brown hair and blue eyes—certainly not travelling on his muscle; all nervous intensity and feeling, a perfect enthusiast in his work, eager of face and voice, full of magnetism. Gardner, shorter, stouter, with amber eyes and hair like gold, less quick and tense, yet made of the stuff that *takes* and holds on.

I remember that after supper when we were camping at timber line, Gardner took one of his instruments and trotted up the side of the mountain to make some observations. He *expected* to be gone half an hour, and *was* gone, by reason of the clouds, nearer three hours, " but," as he quietly said when he came back, speaking of the clouds, " I conquered them at last."

I looked at him, and at all the little party, with ardent curiosity and admiration, braving rain, snow, sleet, hail, hunger, thirst, exposure, bitter nights, snowy climbs, dangers of death—sometimes a score on a single mountain—for the sake not of a so-called great cause, nor in hot blood, but with still patience and unwearied energy for an abstract science—no more, since the majority cannot work even for fame.

We sat around the great fire that was kept

heaped with the whole trunks of dead trees, and watched the splendors of sun-setting till they were all gone, and, these vanished, still sat on by the blazing fire circled by the solemn stately majesties, talking of many things—strange stories of adventure in mountain and gorge, climbs through which a score of times life had been suspended simply on strength of fingers, or nice poise on a hand-ledge thrust out into eternity, wild tales of frontier struggles—intricacies of science, discussions of human life and experience in crowded cities, devotion and enthusiasm as shown in *any* cause—all things, in fact, that touch the brain and soul, the heart and life, of mortals who really *live*, and do not merely exist.

A talk worth climbing that height to have and to hold.

One that was renewed two days later when, the mountain being "done," we found ourselves in Este's Park at "Evans's," in front of a crackling wood fire, with time a plenty for confabulation, a confabulation that was made more "pecooliar" by the presence of "Rocky Mountain Jim," who, having peregrinated up to see us, sat contentedly and looked at us with his one bright eye, finally in quaint language and with concise vividness narrating many a tale of bear and other desperate fights, one of which had two years before nearly ended his days—had broken his right arm, stove in three ribs, torn out his left eye, and "chawed" him up generally, and yet left spirit and grit enough to tell a good story well and to get through a close shave bravely.

LXIV.

Did *I* tell them of queer people and strange experiences?

Yes, indeed, did I.

Can I recall them now?

No—yes. *One* I remember, because it was the very most inexplicable affair that ever befell—no, did not befall—but that ever came to me "second-hand, almost as good as new."

Found myself one day at a certain town, with "no connection" till five of the afternoon—a train that *might* make sixteen miles an hour with ninety-six miles to get over. Due on the platform at 7.30. *That* wouldn't do. So of course I had to have a "special."

Place and time—Central Iowa, some years ago. Country, just flat plain, not the rolling prairie land lying farther west; no towns, few villages, fenceless, treeless; a speck of any thing easily seen afar had any speck existed.

Even the ties were without incident. One after another, one after another, all alike—same length, striking family resemblance, lying on the even ground without so much as a ditch at the side to break the monotony.

Nothing of interest without, so I turned my eyes to inspect what might be found within. They are generally wide open when they are to look at machines or machinists.

I have travelled behind engines and on them by thousands, and have walked about and questioned and gazed and examined them pretty thoroughly, but always with fresh wonder and admiration. Strong as Titans, obedient as slaves—simple, complicated—helpful, merciless—beautiful, yet terrible.

And I never look at them without wondering what manner of world this will be when some one learns how to utilize not one hundred, nor fifty, but even fifteen per cent of steam.

As to their manipulators: fools don't abound among them. A man needs brains and logic to be a good machinist. I like to watch a first-class one listen to an argument on a subject with which he may be ever so unfamiliar. He sees the flaws, and knows where the screws are loose, and the sequence is broken, and the point overlooked or bunglingly made, better—half the time—than the combatants, though they be no mean ones.

If a man *knows* a machine he knows how to argue from cause to effect step by step of the way, and he isn't easily "bamboozled," and there's precious little "nonsense" about him.

My engineer was one of the right sort. A clear-eyed, intelligent, wide-awake young fellow from New England—the last man in the world you would suspect of either drink or superstitious flim-flams.

He was explaining to me some of the mechanism, when, with his right hand on the lever, he suddenly paused, threw himself half out of the little window, gazed a moment up the track, then, turning away his head with his left hand thrust before it as though shutting out some awful vision, drove on.

There was no mistaking the attitude and its meaning.

" You have run over some one here," said I.

" Yes—no—I don't know," he answered.

His fireman seemed to notice neither action nor

answer. I gazed at both with amazement akin to horror. "Am I rushing through space forty miles an hour in the keeping of two madmen?" thought I. "Let us see."

"You don't know?"

"I don't wonder you look," said he, "and ask too. Will you just kindly oblige me by telling if you saw any thing off at the right?"

"Nothing," said I, "but open plain."

"Nor ahead of us?"

"Nothing but level track."

"Nor behind us? Did you look back?"

"Yes, I looked back. There was nothing but track and plain."

"I knew it," said he, "knew it just as well before I asked as afterward, but couldn't help asking. Do you think that's queer?"

"I think *you* are *troubled*. That is more to the purpose. Do you mind my asking *what* has troubled you?"

"*Do* I mind? Don't I just want to tell you and see what *you* can make of it;" and he drew his hand over his forehead and across his clear eyes as though "it" were a nightmare that threatened to *un*make him. "It beats me."

"I wouldn't let it," smiling to cheer his distressed face. "You are too broad-shouldered to stand that sort of treatment from any thing," at which he laughed a little, and the fireman encouragingly remarked, "You just pitch in, Ned;" and Ned "pitched in."

"As for a story—it isn't much of a story you'll say—but—well! You see as I was coming down the road the other day—a good two weeks ago now—a road I've been over hundreds of times and know every foot of it, I saw, off there at the right, instead of that pancake region, regular hilly country, wild and green-looking, plenty of trees, and among them, on top of a sort of ridge, there was a shambling tavern painted red.

"It was growing dusky, and I could see lights in the tavern, and hear loud voices laughing and rowing. Directly a fellow came plunging out of the door with his hat off, a flannel shirt unbuttoned at the throat, and one sleeve loose and hanging, holding a whiskey-bottle. He reeled down the hill, stumbled and stumbled, struck his foot against a log near the bottom, and pitched forward into the ditch and half across the track.

"I saw what was coming, and had whistled down brakes and reversed the engine. The man could have got on to his feet easy enough if it hadn't been for his cursed whiskey-bottle; but he grabbed it, and held it up so as to save it, and couldn't get his balance of course without both hands, and so pitched forward again, this time flat across the rails and we went over him.

"It was all done in a minute, you see, and the train stopped, and I, staring at Jim here, and he at me.

"'What did you do *that* for?' said Jim, 'jerking her up like that for nothing.'

"'My God! man, run over a human creature, and mash the breath out of him, and then ask what I stop the train for?'

"'Run over a man!' cried Jim. 'Are you crazy or drunk?' but I didn't wait to answer. I streaked up the track to where the conductor was out, and the brakesmen, and the passengers all had their heads out of the windows, and Jim after me, and everybody wanting to know what was the matter, and there—well! *you* know just as well as I, there was the open country and the track all flat as my hand, and nothing else near or far to be seen.

"Drunk? No, I wasn't drunk. I don't drink—ever. And it happened just so?" turning to Jim.

"Just—exactly—so," assented the sooty fireman.

"Yes, just, exactly so," echoed the engineer, "and just exactly so I've seen it every day—and *done* it, regular, since then. And I can't stand it much longer. I've got to quit. Look at that"—holding up his strong hand that was shaking in a way that didn't belong to its muscles, nor to the clear blue eyes that had no drink nor craze in them. "Maybe I can make a change with a friend of mine who wants to come west. Any way, I'm going to get out of here, lively."

I sat and pondered.

"Do you believe me?" said he.

"Believe you? Of course I do. I'm not a fool. I know when a man has truth in his face, and you've got truth in yours—voice, too, for that matter."

He smiled and thrust out his grimy fist. "I'd like to shake hands with you for that—if you don't care."

"But I *do* care," said I, smiling in turn. So we shook hands.

"Can you explain it?"

"No—no more than I can tell you how a flower grows."

We reached our destination and each went his and her way, and so far as I knew there was an end of mystery and explanation.

Five years afterward I was at New Brunswick aiming for the ten o'clock train to Philadelphia.

"Drawing-room car?" called I, as I ran down the long dark platform.

"Drawing-room car this way!" was shouted from the rear blackness.

"Ah, is it you, Miss Dickinson? Plenty of room to-night," and I scrambled in.

About every official and employee on the road knows me. So I turned to see with *which* conductor I was going over, but did not recognize him.

"You don't know me?"

"No," said I, yet found something familiar in face or voice. "You are a new man?"

"Yes," he answered.

"Let me see! Let me see!" thought I. I don't like to be thwarted. I always remember people's faces and always forget their names—I could forget my own—" *Who* is he? When, where did I ever travel with him?"

"You were not a *conductor* when I saw you before. I am sure of *that*," I ventured.

He laughed at my puzzled face and answered, "You're right there."

All at once I placed him.

"Ah!" cried I, "how's the ghost?"

The man had a fine ruddy color, but he turned pale at that—pale as this paper.

"Why, you don't mean that any thing did *really* ever come of it?"

"Yes, but I do."

"What?"

"Well! I'll tell you all in a breath—*that's* the best way, and I don't like talking about it. You know I wanted to get away? Yes. Well, I got my transfer, came to the Philadelphia and Erie road, and my friend went west.

"Maybe I didn't draw a long breath as I got under way that first day, and thought I'd left my bugaboo so far behind me. Every thing about me was so different from what I had quitted, it made me feel like a new man. You know the country the Philadelphia and Erie runs through?"

"I know it. Beautiful, fresh and hilly, and full of streams, with a rough-looking road and curving truck."

"Just so," he assented, "and I went along it cheerful as a cricket, looking at every thing and full of interest till toward nightfall—and then—well!—I shut my eyes and drove ahead. What else could I do? but my fireman was dragging at the rope like mad, and cursing me, and the train was jarring and jolting, and presently stopped."

"What did you do *that* for?" said I.

"'My God, man,' cried he, 'run over a human creature, and mash the breath out of him, and then ask what I stop the train for—are you drunk or crazy?' and he plunged off and I after him.

"I didn't expect to see any thing, but, as I came up the road—off at the left—at the right, you see, as the train ran—there was a bit of hill, and a shambling old red tavern, with some lights shining, on top of it, and a ditch at the bottom, and a lot of people with the conductor and passengers gathered about something on the road, and as I came up—there was the man with his hat off, and his open shirt, and the whiskey bottle in his hand, across the track—dead."

LXV.

Well, we told our stories, and talked our talk far into the night, and having slept the sleep of the just, on beds of deliciously sweet hay, went our way thereafter to "fresh fields and pastures new," each holding its own pleasure or delight. Even the mining towns had their own special interest, though mining towns are *not* absolutely lovely.

Perched on the side of a mountain, with cabins built near the mouth of a "claim," or tunnel, or prospect hole, these exhausted or abandoned, the cabins abandoned with them, and others built at fresh centres of labor, making, of themselves alone, a scene of desolation.

Diggings here, there, and everywhere, rocks blasted, the whole surface of the earth thrown up, water sluiced over this point and that to wash away the precious specks, leaving the face of nature bare to the bone—ugly stones and boulders and loose gravel baking in the sun.

Machinery in use and machinery idle and rusting, quartz mills actively running, and quartz mills weather-beaten and in ruins. The streets long narrow alleys, steep as the mountains themselves, one above another, like birds' trails—hot, dusty, dirty. Endless store of "saloons" gaping on all sides. Nothing special to admire save a deal of generous and whole-souled—if rough—human nature.

And the mines—those silver mines—had their charm too.

Let me see—what was the one at Central City? —the "Bob Tail"—that we travelled into through two thousand feet of main tunnel and branch? The passage-way just about high enough for us to stand upright, wet at the sides, wet underfoot, a little tramway for the toy cars and their donkeys serving to keep our feet from the worst of the puddles. A sunshine "hot as an oven," blazing without; within, an air cold and forbidding as the grave, a blackness so dense that for a long time our candles made no perceptible mark on the gloom, looking like glimmering sparks set in ebony. Advancing, it was to find added warmth, in the heart of the rock uncomfortable heat, and, as our eyes accustomed themselves to the gloom and the candlelight, to a tramp that was not absolutely guided by faith alone.

The day "shift" was going off, and the night "shift" coming on, and we met the miners journeying outward to fresh air and home. If it were but a single man the noise of approaching footsteps sounded like the reverberation of cannon. *That* we would hear, by and by a glimmer would begin to shine, and as it drew near a spectre would be revealed—a really ghostly sight. The men work in linen over-alls and rubber boots. These and their faces completely coated with the mixture made by the wet rock-dust, the blackness of "giant powder," and the silvery whiteness of the ore giving them in the dim light the effect of creatures from another world, and terrifying ones at that.

I believe I have recalled and recorded this special mine because of a small experience that seems commonplace enough in the telling, but that made upon me a profound impression in the acting.

Climbing up a long ladder to look at the stalactite wonders of one of the chambers worked out from the main "lead," we were for a moment in absolute darkness, the candles blown out, and our guide delayed in striking a light. Standing perfectly still, with suspended breath, I heard, through the Stygian gloom, something like the pulse of an enormous heart, and presently, with an appalling clearness and loudness, six strokes sounded. Nothing but the ticking and striking of a clock, but it seemed like the voice of eternity.

LXVI.

Alas, that "sweet things are so fleet!" Alas, that a summer in Colorado ever has to end! Alas, that promises are so often made, even to oneself, only to be broken! When I was leaving that enchanted land, I pledged myself to return to its dear delight with another June, so alone finding courage to tear myself from its ineffable embrace, going from it with so heavy a heart and such dim eyes as prevented a smile at any atrocity or absurdity by the way until I was almost at my journey's end, and then I *had* to laugh.

LXVII.

The conductor who was running us into New York had evidently not travelled enough to acquire good manners. In his case an acquisition greatly needed to cloak ingrained deficiencies, since nature had endowed him with a very bad temper and an exceedingly gruff voice.

A "lone lorn" woman, looking anxious and uncomfortable, and starting up with each call of the brakeman—a call that, as usual, might as well have been made in Choctaw for any information it conveyed, one name sounding like any other name, and all of the names sounding like confusion—at last mustered courage to inquire of the conductor *what* was the place we had just passed, and *when* we would reach so and so.

"Why didn't you listen?" answered he of the gruff voice. "The town's just been called. Haven't you any ears? *I* don't know when we get to so and so—d'ye take me for a time-table?"

The timid woman manifestly had both a temper and a "gift of speech" under provocation, for she responded quickly, "Yes, I've got ears—better than your tongue, too. And I take you for a beast."

It was something to remember—the face of that conductor as he walked away. Judging by its expression I suspect he answered *all* queries of whatever import that by chance were addressed to him through the next four-and-twenty hours.

And the man himself deserved to be marked, for in all my journeyings over tens—no, hundreds of thousands of miles, with railway officials to be numbered by regiments, it was one of the exceedingly few rude returns I ever heard made, to questions some of which might test the patience of Job himself.

Out of the entire army I have not seen a score of train-conductors who were not ready and willing to give or to secure all the information, and bestow all the help that ignorance or helplessness or need might require, and, as a rule, with a patience and good temper that neither heat nor dust nor cold nor sleeplessness nor fatigue could obliterate. Let it stand to their credit as the testimony of "one who knows."

I am writing it here in New York, at the end of my ragged register of people and places, while the summer grows apace and I still have not decided where to go.

Who can tell me?

www.ingramcontent.com/pod-product-compliance
Lightning Source LLC
Chambersburg PA
CBHW031339230426
43670CB00006B/384